Dear Dad,

I love you very much! God Bless.

Please take of yourself.

Love Rina 05/2006

QUEEN MARY

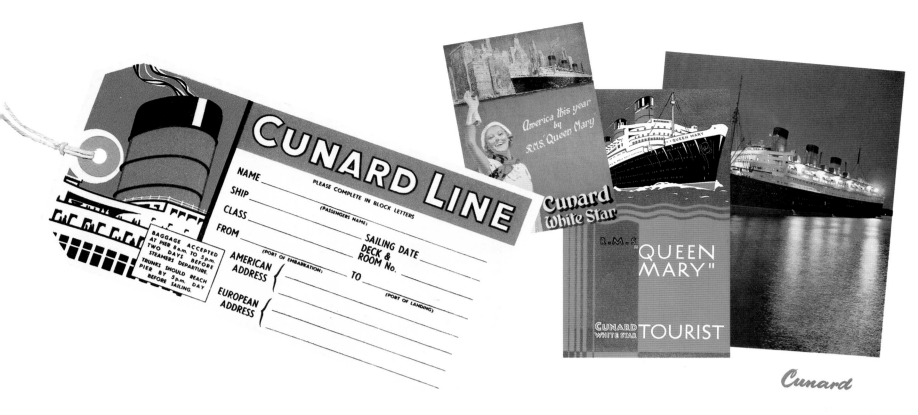

QUEEN MARY

JAMES STEELE

Above A *Queen Mary* match-book kept as a souvenir of a memorable voyage.

Below The *Queen Mary* steams on her last ever voyage towards Long Beach Harbour, where she remains in mummified retirement.

The beloved *New Yorker* writer E B White once wrote: 'I heard the *Queen Mary* blow one mid-night and the sound carried the whole history of departure, longing and loss.' It was a familiar summons to sea that I could hear quite clearly from my 78th Street Manhattan garden.

Although she boasted the slightly larger *Queen Elizabeth* as a near sister, *Queen Mary* remains what the British call a 'one-off', one of a distinctive kind. A ship for all seasons, she offered superlative peacetime luxury as well as commodious reliability during hostilities.

She enjoyed an enviable service longevity, 31 years from her maiden voyage in June 1936 until her withdrawal in the fall of 1967. Conceived by Britain's Cunard Line and wrought by Clydebank Scots, she embarked more Americans than any other nationality, including hundreds of thousands of khaki-clad, involuntary passengers who endured the crowded discomfort of wartime passage. Once she ceased sailing, as though loath to abandon her Yankee predilection, *Queen Mary* 'finished with engines' as an anachronistic

addition to Long Beach's waterfront. By 1998, the great Cunarder will have been tied up moribund in California for exactly as many years as she thundered across the world's oceans.

James Steele, an architect by training and a keen observer by instinct, has produced an exhaustive history of the vessel, a must for marine and architectural historians as well as ocean-liner buffs everywhere; 'definitive' is a risky qualifier but one that legitimately describes this volume. The author treads maritime holy ground: no more universally beloved vessel ever sailed the North Atlantic and no more ambitious a floating preservation has ever been attempted.

Predictably, the Long Beach results are mixed. Beset by debt and often misguided renovation, *Queen Mary* soldiers on as a hotel, convention centre and, for contemporary Americans, faded icon of an increasingly remote past. The logistical and economic demands of preservation on this scale are overwhelming. Most of her furniture has gone; the great suites of promenade-deck public rooms make do with stacking hotel chairs

and banquet tables; alien restaurants and souvenir shops crowd her upper decks; spurious pop-historical videos divert touring visitors. For these day-trippers – *Queen Mary*'s simulacrum passenger legatees – the vessel through which they tramp remains an echoing, incomprehensible relic, a pale shadow of her former seagoing self.

Nevertheless – and this is the miracle – she is still with us. My favourite view of her is from afar, a hinterland vision glittering through Long Beach's relentless smog or, seaward, hauntingly floodlit at night. That imperious funnel trio, once familiar from Manhattan to Southampton and Capetown to Sydney, remains as was; years of troubled Californian exile have not changed that.

But since so much inside *Queen Mary* has been irretrievably lost, Steele's volume is mandatory reading for the serious student of Cunard's history. He tells us not only how *Queen Mary* originally looked but also why, documenting the social and decorative forces that shaped her as well as the mid-thirties taste that her designers embraced and often saw rejected. Thanks to

the author's scrupulous research, we can embark on the original, within that fragrant, creaking realm of korkoid, lumiline, beeswax, wood panelling and string orchestras that so entranced and cosseted three decades' worth of North Atlantic travellers.

I often wonder about passenger sensitivity to the interiors they enjoy. Cocooned within those heaving, glistening chambers, how many appreciate the exacting toil of architect and designer? Probably not more than one in a thousand. But thanks to James Steele's meticulous and articulate history, *Queen Mary*'s fabric has been beautifully rewoven, preserved in a way that Long Beach's city fathers have never achieved.

John Maxtone-Graham
At sea, April 1995

Number 534

For ages you were rock, far below light,
Crushed, without shape, earth's unregarded bone.
Then Man in all the marvel of his might
Quarried you out and burned you from the stone.

Then, being pured to essence, you were nought
But weight and hardness, body without nerve;
Then Man in all the marvel of his thought,
Smithied you into form of leap and curve;

And took you, so, and bent you to his vast,
Intense great world of passionate design,
Curve after changing curving, braced and masst
To stand all tumult that can tumble brine,

And left you, this, a rampart of a ship,
Long as a street and lofty as a tower,
Ready to glide in thunder from the slip
And shear the sea with majesty of power.

I long to see you leaping to the urge
Of the great engines, rolling as you go,
Parting the seas in sunder in a surge,
Shredding a trackway like a mile of snow

With all the wester streaming from your hull
And all gear twanging shrilly as you race,
And effortless above your stern a gull
Leaning upon the blast and keeping place.

May shipwreck and collision, fog and fire,
Rock, shoal and other evils of the sea,
Be kept from you; and may the heart's desire
Of those who speed your launching come to be.

A poem specially written by the Poet Laureate,
John Masefield, to celebrate the launch of the
Queen Mary on 26 September 1934. As yet
unnamed she was still identified by her shipyard
designation: Job Number *534*.

O f all the Cunard Line's magnificent ships, perhaps the stately *Queen Mary* managed best to transcend the utilitarian associations of transatlantic travel. She became famous for her speed, elegant configuration and high standard of finish and accommodation as soon as she was put into service.

With her maiden voyage on 27 May 1936, the sleek new liner provided a tangible symbol of the end of the Depression

To celebrate the maiden voyage of the *Queen Mary*, Cunard published a 'Book of Comparisons' in the United States intended to spark the American public's imagination.

that had threatened her completion, making the event a great national occasion.

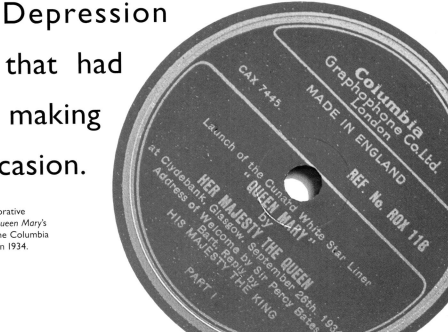

Opposite The *Queen Mary* in dry dock in Southampton shortly after her maiden arrival in her home port. Accounts of the new liner were coloured with superlatives: she was the 'stateliest', the 'sleekest' and soon to prove the 'fastest' ship afloat.

Right A commemorative recording of the *Queen Mary*'s launch issued by the Columbia Gramophone Co in 1934.

In the early 1930s, the *Queen Mary* represented a vast and brave undertaking, a ship-building challenge of unprecedented proportions and a statement of faith in British design and engineering skills. She was to be the largest, the fastest and the finest liner ever built, the proud new flagship of the Cunard Line, which since its founding in the nineteenth century by Samuel Cunard, had been Britain's pre-eminent steamship company, representing the acme of service and style on the transatlantic run.

Right The *Britannia* pioneered Samuel Cunard's transatlantic service in the 1840s. One of four sister Cunarders it helped to gain the line a reputation for reliability and safety second to none.

Below A view of the *Queen Mary* at sea from the 'Book of Comparisons'. Alongside her, drawn to scale, are the *Britannia* and Columbus' three ships the *Nina*, *Pinto* and *Santa Maria* which Cunard boasted could be accommodated in the super-liner's main foyer and restaurant.

Cunard's first steamship, the *Britannia*, left Liverpool in the summer of 1840, carrying passengers and mail between England and Boston, and Halifax, Nova Scotia, making the journey twice each month under Admiralty contract. The *Britannia* and its sister ships, the *Arcadia*, *Caledonia* and *Columbia*, were built on Clydebank in Scotland establishing a tradition that the *Queen Mary* was to continue.

The *Britannia* was tiny, only 230 feet long, 34 feet 6 inches wide at the beam and 22 feet 6 inches at the deepest part of the hold, and would have fitted easily into the *Queen Mary's* spacious cabin-class restaurant. But progressively larger vessels began to appear. The British and American Steam Navigation Company commissioned the *Sirius* in 1837, which was the first ship to cross the Atlantic, under continuous steam power. When the *Sirius* glided into New York harbour on 23 April 1838, having completed a particularly stormy passage in 15 days, at an average speed of 8.2 knots, the race across the North Atlantic, or 'the run', was on, in which high speed was ultimately translated into great wealth for the line that could boast the fastest crossing. Having proven that the run could be made expeditiously and safely, the *Sirius* continued the rush to the water that was formalized by Cunard's contract for the *Britannia*, and the unofficial prize, the 'Blue Riband', for the steamer that managed the fastest crossing became a coveted symbol for the competition that ensued.

When the American magnate Edward Knight Collins founded his line, and built the *Atlantic*, *Pacific*, *Arctic* and *Baltic*, they were acclaimed as much for the amenities they offered their passengers as for their speed, boasting smoking rooms, bathrooms, a barber's shop and heated public rooms, including a dining 'saloon', drawing room and spacious staterooms, all fitted out in exotic woods. Averaging 11.75 knots between them, Collins' initial quartet of ships posed a serious threat to the speed records set by Cunard, and the battle between the two companies see-sawed back and forth for more than a decade. But disaster befell the Collins Line when, in 1854, the *Arctic* collided with the French steamer *Vesta*

In the early part of this century, the power and might of transatlantic liners was measured as much by their complement of funnels as by sheer tonnage. This advertising poster shows the Cunarder *Aquitania*, a reassuringly well-equipped four-stacker, which entered Atlantic service in May 1914, shortly before the outbreak of World War I.

Right The *Lusitania* pulls into Cunard's 14th-Street pier in New York to be met by a sea of horse-drawn cabs. Known popularly as 'The Lucy' she set the Atlantic record on her second voyage, with an average speed of 24 knots. Her sister ship, the *Mauretania,* took this record from her a few months later beating her time by 21 minutes, making the crossing from New York in four days, 22 hours and 29 minutes.

Below A ceramic-tile depiction of the *Mauretania* against the backdrop of Manhattan in the Marine Grill Restaurant, New York.

60 miles south of Cape Race and sank with all its 391 passengers, including the proprietor's wife and two children. This tragic event signalled the beginning of the end of this particular American challenge, and underlined Cunard's continuing emphasis on reliability rather than speed. It was decided, for example, not to go full-speed for the

Blue Riband on the *Queen Mary*'s maiden voyage. Following the loss of the *Arctic*, Cunard was quick to boast that it had made more than 7,000 transatlantic passages between 1840 and 1854, carrying in excess of 100,000 passengers, without loss of life or property. This position, on which Samuel Cunard had built his entire reputation, continued to be the company's unspoken policy. Speed, and the profits it brought, were important; but safety, which ensured passenger loyalty, was paramount.

From the outbreak of the American Civil War in 1861 until the turn of the century, Britain's shipowners, builders and designers monopolized the North Atlantic run, with national companies such as Cunard, White Star and Inman competing amongst themselves for the Blue Riband. In this 'Golden Age', as one historian has described it, development was marked by the change from iron to steel for the construction of hulls, from paddlewheels to single and twin-screw propellers

Left The *Normandie* in dock in the mid-1930s. One of the most graceful and elegantly-appointed Atlantic liners ever built, she entered service in 1935. The French ship rivalled the *Queen Mary* in both size and speed but was popularly judged to have the edge in terms of sheer *élan*.

Below An advertisement for the Manganese Bronze and Brass Company's propellers as fitted to the *Queen Mary* and a host of predecessors including the *Normandie* and *Mauretania*. The *Queen Mary*'s profile has been exaggerated for dramatic effect; in reality the *Normandie* was 11 feet longer above the waterline.

and from single to compound steam-engines: 'They were the years when passenger accommodation scaled new heights of luxury and when the American packet ships ... were finally eclipsed.'

At the end of this period, however, the Germans stepped up their efforts to compete on the transatlantic run; the maiden voyage of the *Kaiser Wilhelm der Grosse* by the Norddeutscher Lloyd Line on 19 September 1897, was distinguished by a crossing from the Needles at Southampton to Sandy Hook, New York in five days 22 hours 30 minutes at an average speed of 21.39 knots. This initiative elicited a determined response from the Cunard Company, and in 1907 the *Lusitania* and *Mauretania* made their début, built by John Brown on Clydebank and Swan Hunter and Wigham Richardson on Tyneside, respectively.

The *Lusitania* on her second passage from Liverpool to New York, recaptured the Blue

THE SHIPBUILDER AND MARINE ENGINE-BUILDER

The M.B. & B. Co's MANGANESE BRONZE PROPELLERS

MAKE HISTORY

1875   Mr. F. M. Parsons Invents Manganese Bronze.
1880   H.M.S. "COLOSSUS" 1st vessel fitted.
1889   PARIS, NEW YORK

CAMPANIA, LUCANIA

KAISER WILHELM

DEUTSCHLAND

KRONPRINZ WILHELM

MAURETANIA

BREMEN, EUROPA

CONTE DI SAVOIA

NORMANDIE

1936   QUEEN MARY

THE MANGANESE BRONZE & BRASS COMPANY LTD
CAXTON HOUSE, WESTMINSTER, LONDON, S.W.1.

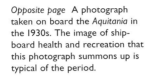

Riband for Britain, with a time of four days, 19 hours 52 minutes and an average speed of 24 knots, slightly shy of the 24.5 knots she had been designed to maintain. The *Mauretania* bettered this time in November 1907, by a slim but decisive margin of 24 minutes, beginning the battle for record times which the two ships were to continue until the beginning of World War I. A year after the war began, on 7 May 1915, the *Lusitania* was sunk by a German submarine off the coast of Southern Ireland, tragically ending the legend of this pre-eminent pair.

Transatlantic traffic was slow to recover after host-ilities ceased in 1918. An Act of Congress limiting immigration into the United States re-duced passenger numbers dramatically and forced the shipping lines to rationalize their operations accordingly. By the late twenties a trio of Cunarders, *Mauretania*, *Aquitania* and *Berengaria*, had established a regular pattern of post-war passenger service, but 'the queens of the North Atlantic', as they were proudly known, were either approaching middle-age or, in the case of the *Mauretania*, due for retirement; thus leading the company to embark upon an ambitious new strategy which they hoped would help regain the

supremacy it had once taken for granted. The basis of their plan was a reduction of the number of liners operating the weekly Cunard mail service from Southampton to New York from three to two. This had the advantage of cutting costs but also required an increase in size and speed, thus making it possible for the two new ships to carry more passengers, on a regular weekly schedule.

By this time 'tourist-class' accommodation had replaced the loss in steerage revenue as the immi-grant trade to the United States tailed off, and the stakes involved in achieving the speed record were accordingly much higher. In rapid succes-sion, following Germany's introduction of the *Bremen* in 1929 and the *Europa* in 1930, Italy weighed in with its own bid for a share of this tourist market, with the *Conte di Savoia* and the *Rex*, both launched in 1932, as did France with the *Normandie*, in 1935. It was against the

Opposite page A photograph taken on board the *Aquitania* in the 1930s. The image of ship-board health and recreation that this photograph summons up is typical of the period.

Above Shipping companies sought ever newer and more enticing ways to secure passengers on the North Atlantic run, promis-ing them increasingly elaborate sports and recreational facilities among other amenities. The sports deck and lido swimming pool on board the Italian liner *Rex* exemplified this trend. Entering service in 1932, she briefly held the westbound Atlantic speed record in August 1933 only to lose it again to the German liner *Bremen*.

Below left The smoking room on board the *Rex* is depicted in this illustration as if both it and its occupants had been transplanted from the smartest Adriatic resort; french doors lead couples out to the starlit waters beyond the promenade deck.

Below right The contrasting Edwardian pomp of Mewès and Davis' Palladian Lounge on the *Aquitania*. Theatre evenings such as this were common on the largest liners, adding to the required impression of after-dark metropolitan sophistication.

Right Two famous Cunard posters from the 1920s; Kenneth Shoesmith's '*Aquitania* in New York' and Odin Rosenvinge's impression of the *Berengaria* at sea.

Below The 'Hales Trophy', presented by the British Member of Parliament Harold Hales, which in theory at least was presented to the holder of the Atlantic speed record. The first recipients, the *Rex*, *Europa* and *Normandie* were all outshone by the *Queen Mary* although Cunard declined to accept the trophy.

backdrop of this competitive panoply that the *Queen Mary* began to take shape.

As if anticipating the victory that the public felt was sure to come as soon as the *Queen Mary* was finished, a Member of Parliament, Harold Keates Hales, proposed and donated a trophy to commemorate the Blue Riband in a more formal way. The 'Hales Trophy', as it became known, was to be awarded to the ship with the fastest round-trip time across the North Atlantic. Ostentatiously mounted on an onyx base, the trophy comprises various mythological figures supporting a globe that represents the earth; it is garlanded at its base by an enamelled blue ribbon, and enclosed with sculptural and pictorial representations of several of the most memorable winners of the prize, along with fanciful caravels, supposedly implying exploration.

The *Queen Mary*, or job number *534* as she was designated in the shipyard, was envisioned as being nearly three times the size of the 31,938-ton *Mauretania*; almost twice that of the 45,600-ton *Aquitania*; and a third heavier than the 52,000-ton *Berengeria*. Like these three ships, the *Queen Mary* was to be driven by steam turbines. Charles Parsons had dramatically demonstrated the efficiency of the steam turbine, when he unexpectedly raced his *Turbinia* through the assembled fleet at Spithead in 1897. Since 1906 it had been the power plant of choice, for all Cunard ships. The *Mauretania*, *Aquitania* and *Berengeria* had all been capable of 22 to 25 knots (25.3 to 28.8 mph); and now, with the conversion from coal-fired to oil-fired boilers in the 1920s, the psychological stage was set for the design of a liner that could achieve the 28.5-knot average speed necessary to realize Cunard's new

A Cunard publicity poster from the late 1930s showing the *Queen Mary* and her ageing temporary consorts the *Berengaria* and *Aquitania*. In descending order of tonnage, they weighed in at 81,000, 52,000 and 45,600 tons respectively.

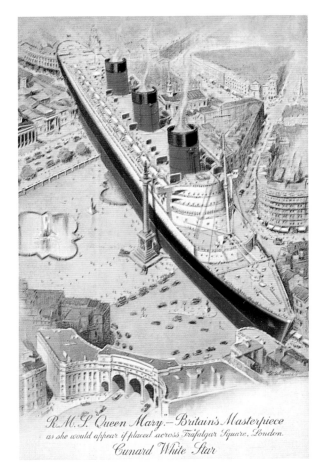

R.M.S. "Queen Mary."—Britain's Masterpiece
as she would appear if placed across Trafalgar Square, London.
Cunard White Star

CHIC
BOAR
609

DETROIT,
PENOBSCOT
557 FEE

PHILADELPHIA
CITY HALL
548 FEET

BOSTON, MAS
CUSTOM HOU!
496 FEET

SEATTLE, WASH.
SMITH TOWER
462 FEET

LOS ANGELES, CAL.
CITY HALL
438 FEET

SAN FRANCISCO, CAL.
RUSS BUILDING
435 FEET

HIBERNIA BANK BUILDING
NEW ORLEANS, LA.
355 FEET.

RHODES-HAVERTY
BUILDING
ATLANTA, GA.
250 FEET

The "QUEEN MARY" MEASU

Above The *Queen Mary* in Trafalgar Square. Countless images of this kind were employed by Cunard to reinforce the fact that the *Queen Mary* was the largest vessel yet built. Compare this view with that of the liner on Fifth Avenue (*page 74*).

Opposite More *Queen Mary* comparisons, this time with some of the world's tallest structures. Longer than the Eiffel Tower is tall, she was only 230 feet shorter than the Empire State Building, her land-bound contemporary.

goal of express transatlantic passenger service by two 80,000-ton vessels with weekly sailing times from two fixed ports. Notwithstanding new developments in turbo-electric and diesel engines which powered some of the world's fastest ships, Cunard took a conservative stance and determined that steam turbine engines would be the most reliable choice. The average speed they chose was the minimum necessary to maintain their weekly schedule on the shortest of the established liner tracks, along the northern Atlantic route used in summer and the southern in winter, with a configuration that would provide the desired mix of cabin-class, tourist-class and third-class accommodation to make the run economically viable.

John Brown and Company had supplied many Cunard liners and was asked to collaborate at an early stage on this new design, which the company stipulated should follow established

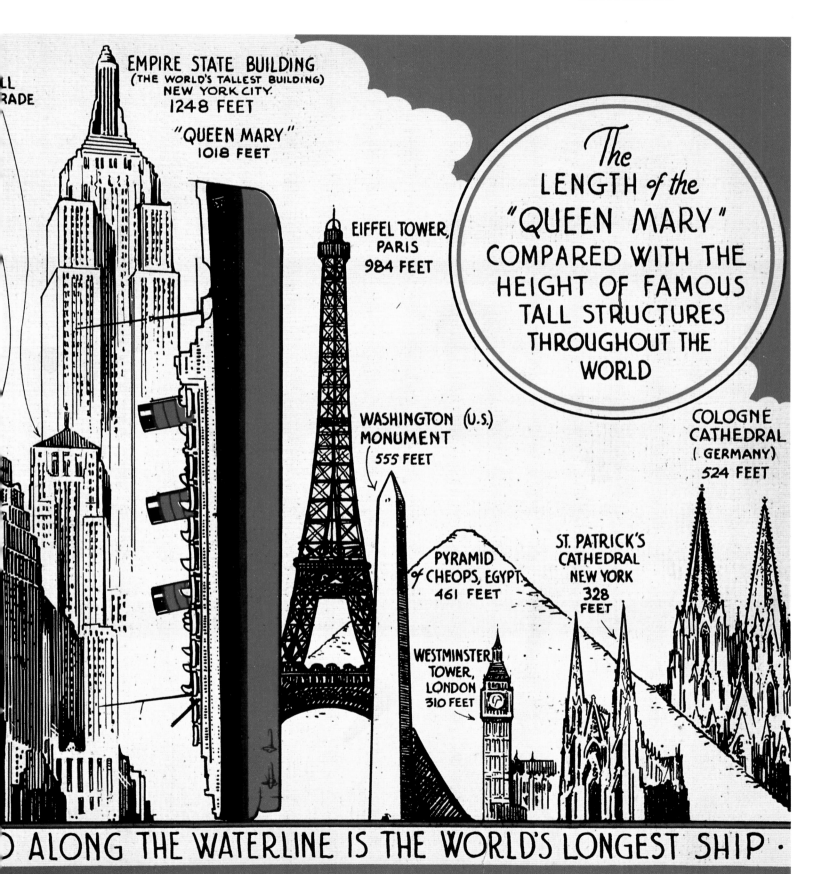

Above The cover of Cunard's house magazine for Christmas 1931 celebrated the construction of the new giant liner. Ironically work was suspended that same month due to the economic emergency caused by the Depression.

Centre On the slipway of John Brown's yard on Clydebank, the *Queen Mary's* after-end framing takes shape, soaring into the sky like the rib cage of some machine-age mammal.

Opposite page Construction work on the hull proceeded rapidly throughout 1931. *Clockwise from top* A view of the stern during shell plating; a section of the hull shoring; the hull plating nears completion; a view of the hull partly framed, with the lower deck levels clearly discernible.

engineering principles rather than speculative initiatives. As the design progressed, 22 successive models, each 200 inches long, were tested in tanks in which artificially-created waves that simulated storm conditions on the North Atlantic were reproduced to scale. Accurate records were kept of the more than 8,000 model trials that were carried out, in which attention mainly focused on minimizing the resistance of the bow through the water and the degree of pitch and roll. Each test was also filmed for cross-comparison with the others. The singularly elegant, sweeping hull profile that ultimately emerged was comprehensively and pragmatically described in *The Shipbuilder and Marine Engine Builder* at the time, which noted that, 'when travelling at speed into a head sea, the vessel will "ride" well and the water will be effectively and naturally thrown clear and thus prevented from breaking on board'. The flared bow and cruiser stern which these tests dictated were the major innovations permitted by a prudent company:

they alone were sufficient to single out *534* from its predecessors, giving it an aspect of refinement and impression of power and speed that even those behemoths lacked.

By December 1930, John Brown had made the substantial renovations necessary to its Clydebank shipyard, and began to lay the keel of *534*'s enormous hull, but the path to the ship's completion would not be a smooth one. Within a year, the economic Depression that had brought America to its knees had spread across the Atlantic, and work on the hull, which had by then risen high enough to create a second horizon along the Clyde, was suspended on 12 December 1931. While this was certainly a disaster for Clydebank, the economic and political reverberations were

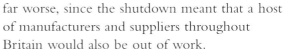

far worse, since the shutdown meant that a host of manufacturers and suppliers throughout Britain would also be out of work.

While the *Queen Mary* was famously to be an 'all-British' ship, she was equally an all-Britain job, relying on a host of suppliers and manufacturers from more than 60 towns and cities. To give several examples: her steel, castings and steering equipment came from Motherwell; her windows from Liverpool; her electrical switchgear from Chester; her electric motors from Brighton; her metalwork and bronze castings from Wolverhampton; her carpets from Kidderminster, Bridgnorth, Halifax and Brighouse; her porcelain and cooking ware from Worcester and her linen from Northern Ireland.

Eventually, after two years of uncertainty and political debate, kept alive largely by the championing of the Clydeside Member of Parliament, David Kirkwood, the British Government approved the £3 million necessary to complete *534* of which £1.5 million was advanced immediately as working capital, with assurances of an additional loan of £5 million if a sister ship were to be built. As part of this contingency plan, it was also stipulated that the White Star Line, owners of the ill-fated *Titanic*, which had a distinguished history of its own since its founding in 1869, should be merged with Cunard. The Board of Trade wisely recognized that many of the White Star liners would soon be obsolete and would also require a government subsidy to replace them. Work on *534*, which had now become the flagship of the newly-reorganized Cunard White Star Line, began again on 3 April 1934, symbolizing in a potent way the end of the crushing grip of the Depression.

The story behind the construction of the ship's hull, which has typically been glossed over in the past in favour of more glamorous aspects of the *Queen Mary*'s history, is in itself an engineering achievement of epic proportions, on a level comparable with that of the Eiffel Tower by AG Eiffel, or the Roebling brothers' Herculean struggle to complete the Brooklyn Bridge.

Beginning with the basic criterion of realizing a ship with a size and speed capable of maintaining a profitable weekly North Atlantic passenger service in tandem with a sister vessel, Cunard and the designers at John Brown under the general direction of the chief Naval Architect, Sir James McNeill, decided that it would have to be in excess of a thousand feet long, carry more than 3,000 passengers, and be able to reach a top speed of 28.5 knots, although the ship eventually far exceeded that.

In keeping with their generally conservative approach, the designers of the *Queen Mary* chose well-established, fundamental methods of determining the stress values that would be permissible

in the structural arrangement of the hull. Such calculations are more difficult in ship construction than in architecture or civil engineering because of the number of unknowns involved. Considering the worst condition of bending to be one in which the vessel would be subjected to a wave with its crest amidships, the engineers were able to determine a workable formula that would balance the hull's longitudinal and trans-

Opposite page Constructing the hull required the co-ordination of countless engineering and manufacturing skills, applied at an unprecedented scale. *Clockwise from top left* The 130-feet-long stem casting assembled at the works of Messrs Thomas Firth & John Brown Ltd of Sheffield; the cast-steel inner propeller shaft brackets which were cast in two sections, each weighing 120 tons; the after-end framing into which these castings would be located taking shape on the slipway.

Above The *Queen Mary*'s stern frame was cast in five sections with an assembled weight of 190 tons. It is shown here at the works of the Darlington Forge from where it was moved by rail to Clydebank.

Left An advertisement placed by Thomas Firth & John Brown Ltd, in the souvenir issue of *The Shipbuilder* published in June 1936 to coincide with the *Queen Mary*'s entry into Atlantic service.

Overleaf For nearly three years, the *Queen Mary*'s silent hull formed a second horizon on Clydebank, dwarfing the works of John Brown and Company where construction had ceased in December 1931. Here, the shipyard workers march back into action after a government subsidy allowed work on the ship to resume in April 1934.

verse strength. This led to a decision to use bulk-heads as a means of strengthening the hull, in a double-shell arrangement, as well as the use of high-elastic-limit steel in the upper parts of the ship, to reduce its weight. Transverse framing was strengthened by subdivisions spaced according to the bending-moment calculations, the spacing between frames becoming progressively narrower toward the ends of the hull. Other arrangements were determined by international conventions of watertightness, established following the calamity that befell the *Titanic*. The construction of the hull was well described in *The Shipbuilder*:

'Due to the exceptional nature of the problem, the usual conception of side framing (say, channels with occasional webs) was deemed inadequate, and closely spaced webs (at every third frame in the lower part of the structure) constituting an integral part of the framing arrangements have been incorporated. They are, in general, 48 inches deep below E deck, and 36 inches deep in the 'tween decks; while in many cases they take the form of partial bulkheads of considerable extent. The intermediate frames are of channel section, 12 inches deep in the way of the oil breakers, and 11 inches deep in the 'tween decks. The frame spacing over the greater length of the vessel is

36 inches. Towards the end of the vessel, the spacing is progressively reduced to 24 inches.'

The relative depth of the webs used, of three and four feet, gives some idea of the massive scale of the hull structure, which began to resemble the skeletal thorax of some species of prehistoric leviathan as it rose on its slipway beside the Clyde. The spine of the skeleton is a six-foot-deep girder that runs the entire length of the ship, which has the outside skin of the keel attached to its bottom flange, and the inner skin, of 1.20 inch steel plate, riveted to the top. At the landward end of the slipway, the keel rose 27 feet above the ground, necessitating the construction of a steel platform that bridged over a rail line specifically built to deliver materials to the site. In stark contrast, rough-hewn logs were used to shore up the entire length of the hull as it rose off the slipway, with steel scaffolding rising up slowly around it as the external shellplating progressed.

The construction of the *Queen Mary*'s hull was an extraordinary engineering achievement, generating a plethora of mind-boggling statistics; for example: over ten million rivets were used to secure its steel plates, each one hammered home by hand using 'Thor' pneumatic riveting hammers. Naturally, the *Queen Mary* 'Book of Comparisons' could not resist the temptation to give this incredible statistic an illustrative twist, piling these very real rivets into an imaginary pyramid.

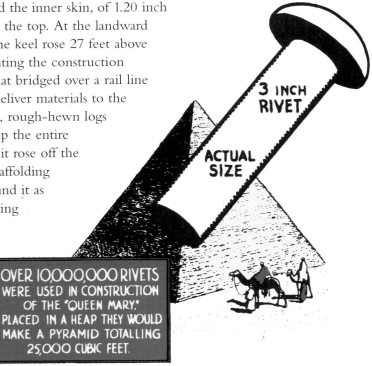

Above The *Queen Mary*'s propelling machinery and boilers were assembled in the John Brown works on Clydebank, the aggregate power plant being arranged in ten separate watertight engine-room compartments. Here, the arrangement of turbines and gearing for the starboard outer propeller shaft is seen from its forward end prior to installation.

The steel castings, produced by the Darlington Forge, were larger than any that had previously been manufactured for maritime use, even in such enormous vessels as the *Mauretania* and *Aquitania*. To accommodate the castings, the forge had to build four new brick-lined watertight tanks, to hold the various moulds that were required. The larger castings involved a complex and lengthy process of simultaneously drawing off molten steel from two separate furnaces, which each yielded 60 tons at one time. In spite of the seemingly implacable and precise nature of the technology involved, there was also a great degree of craftsmanship required in the production of these castings, as well as in the plating of the hull. In the creation of the patterns for the five sections of the stern frame, for example, which extends from the keel to the top of the hull, allowance had to be made for the shrinkage that would occur as the steel cooled, and the settling of the castings, so that no flaws would result. The stem casting, which is nearly 130 feet long, has a U-shaped cross section that varies from four inches at the

base of the U to little more than one inch thick at the flanges, and is typical of the balance between industrial precision and human intuition that characterizes the workmanship on the hull. This is especially apparent on sighting down the length of the ship, where the subtle aesthetics of its incremental curvature become most obvious.

The first rivet was driven into the hull by Donald Skiffington, the shipyard manager, who had begun as an apprentice on Clydebank. Millions of rivets were eventually required to join the steel plating and face the hull ribs in order to achieve that graceful, and decidedly unmechanized, curve. Extreme care was also taken in the extensive amount of welding, cutting, grinding, drilling and brazing that was required to form the ship's external skin into one uniform, monogenic and watertight surface. Indeed, the impressions of one excited reporter written shortly before the launch of the as yet unnamed ship, bear repeating at length to convey the enormity of this undertaking:

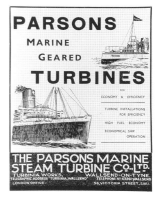

'Rounding a corner of a dour building you get your first sudden view of her – a monstrous bow which rears into the sky. Another hundred yards, another corner and there she is – 1,018 feet in length, and about 135 feet high; trussed in a forest of timber, with a roar of vigorous young life vibrating from her immense dark red body. Of course you stand transfixed and gaping, for quite a time. The mind has nothing to work on to attune itself to such a spectacle. It is impossible for any but marine engineers to appreciate the extent of the matter except with the help of mental image. So, to enable you more fully to understand the scope of this maritime achieve-ment, here are two simple comparisons. She is exactly the same length as the first hole at Prestwick golf course – 339 yards. And if you could stand her up on one end alongside the Eiffel Tower in Paris, she would top that structure by 18 feet...

'A number of pictures have been drawn accu-rately to scale for the elucidation of the lay mind.

Above left One of the giant tur-bines being finished and adjusted by hand. Each main turbine set comprised one high-pressure, two intermediate-pressure and one low-pressure turbine work-ing in series. The huge scale of this machinery can be judged from this photograph.

Above An advertisement for Parsons Marine Geared Turbines, as used in the *Queen Mary*.

Left A low-pressure main tur-bine being secured in position in the *Queen Mary*'s engine-room.

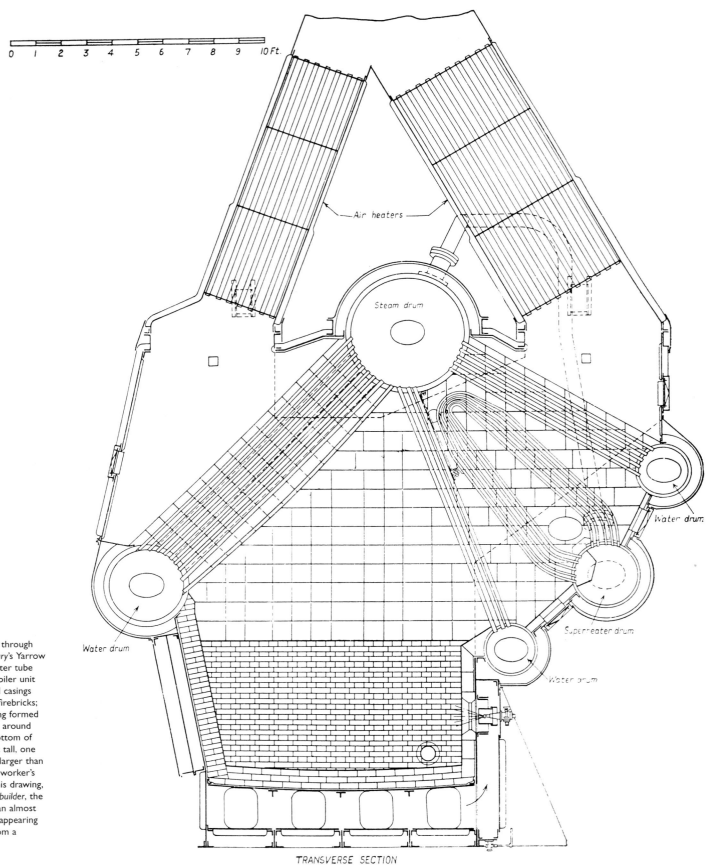

0 1 2 3 4 5 6 7 8 9 10 Ft.

Air heaters

Steam drum

Water drum

Water drum

Superheater drum

Water drum

Water drum

A transverse section through one of the *Queen Mary*'s Yarrow double-flow main water tube boilers. The entire boiler unit was enclosed in steel casings lined internally with firebricks; another outside casing formed a complete air jacket around the furnace at the bottom of the boiler. At 30 feet tall, one of these boilers was larger than the average shipyard worker's terraced house. In this drawing, published in *The Shipbuilder*, the machinery takes on an almost architectural quality, appearing like an illustration from a Futurist manifesto.

TRANSVERSE SECTION

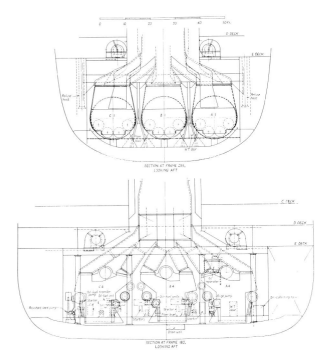

posse of self-contained overalled men to the boat deck, which they are now making. Through an aperture in her side, and then into the tumult! Pneumatic riveting of steel plates emits a high-pitched scream. Hundreds of pneumatic and hydraulic riveters are at work at this moment (the latter with pressure of a ton to the square inch in great lobster-like claws), reverberating through the empty steel shell of the ship, through all her twelve decks, over all her tremendous length…

'Official records have it that into this ship are driven ten million rivets which, if formed into a chain, would reach from London to Newcastle – 270 miles, and collectively weigh 4,000 tons; yet every single rivet has a man's personality stamped into it. It represents his concentration and craftsman's-pride, his tenacity – and his backache.

One such shows her set down in Trafalgar Square, The Nelson Column is on her starboard beam; the crown of Nelson's hat reaches to about the boat deck. Her stern has pushed in the walls of the Garrick Theatre in Charing Cross Road; her port side only just fits alongside St Martin's Church and South Africa House; the National Gallery is severely damaged, and her stem has protruded into Whitehall…

'Other world-famous structures, drawn to scale with her as a background, look puny. The up-raised hand of the Statue of Liberty in New York Harbour would reach only just above the bridge. The tip of the towers of Westminster Abbey would not reach to the top of her mainmast. The head of the Sphinx would be well below the main deck at the stern. The top of the Magdalen Tower at Oxford would only be halfway up her middle funnel. The roof of the Berlin Opera House would just about reach to the deck of the fo'c'sle. And one of the promenade decks is more than twice the length of the facade of Buckingham Palace…

'A high skeleton-framed lift stands alongside the gargantuan structure, and in it you ascend with a

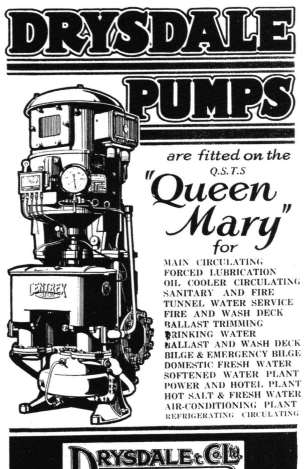

Above left Sections through numbers 1 and 4 boiler rooms showing the general arrangement of the machinery. In all there were five boiler rooms – four main and one auxiliary. Number 1 housed three double-ended Scotch boilers. In numbers 2, 3, 4 and 5 boiler rooms, six Yarrow water-tube boilers were fitted in each compartment, making a total of 24 main boilers.

Above An advertisement placed by the Yarrow Company of Glasgow in the commemorative June 1936 issue of *The Shipbuilder*.

Left Drysdale & Company, also of Glasgow, supplied pumps, air-conditioning plant and hot salt and fresh water-supply equipment for the *Queen Mary*.

Right An advertisement placed by G & J Weir Ltd of Glasgow proclaiming their contribution to the *Queen Mary*'s power plant, and the merits of the Weir 'closed feed system' designed to protect boilers and steam lines against corrosion due to gases in solution in the feed.

Below A longitudinal elevation and plan of the main and auxiliary boiler rooms showing the general arrangement of the *Queen Mary*'s 24 main boilers. The six boilers at the forward end of the ship were slightly smaller than those aft and were designed to suit the narrowing width of the hull. The forward, midships and after boiler groupings correspond to each of the ship's three funnels respectively.

Opposite page A boiler flue casing awaiting installation; the stencilled legend 'port inner aft end' denotes its destination.

This was manifest to all observers on Clydeside throughout the eighteen months of careful labour; and though rich carpets, lustrous enamel and soft upholstery will hide many of those rivets, that simple fact will remain her pre-eminent attribute through all her triumphant days...

'Hereabouts the bones and sinews have been already fashioned, and embellishment – eighteen months of further craftsmanship – is not yet due. But in those interminable corridors, and between the gaunt red rivet-studded walls, you gain some appreciation of the steelwork statistics. You are not so surprised now on recollecting that the steel plating of this ship would pave the main road

from London to Nottingham and would entirely cover St James's Park and The Mall. The red walls have little guiding placards here and there, telling you where you are...

'You can examine the tremendous spaces set aside for the kitchens and their ancillary service rooms. In the first-class lounge the space is such that nine double-decked passenger omnibuses placed abreast, with three 'Royal Scot' engines superimposed on their roofs, could pass under the arch formed by its roof and walls. Here and there on your journey you see smaller spaces – little canyons between steep steel cliffs – and you are puzzled. They are for some of the 21 electric lifts that will serve the ship's people...

'Twenty seven immense boilers there will be, occupying five rooms; over 2,600 feet of main steam piping will lead from the boilers to the engines. For electric power, seven turbo-generator sets, developing 10,000 kilowatts; the greatest power station afloat, sufficient to supply lighting and public services for a town the size of Brighton. "The propelling machinery," they say, "will consist of a quadruple-screw arrangement of Parson's single-reduction-geared turbines." Yes; but we do not venture a dive into the deep technique of that. What does, however, bring stark reality into the forefront of the mind is the fact that every single one of the 257,000 turbine blades, varying in length from two to 16 inches, will be tested and fitted by hand. Seeing these careful men we know what testing means. By the way, these geared rotary turbines store up sufficient energy to run, like spinning tops, along the road from Liverpool to Manchester...

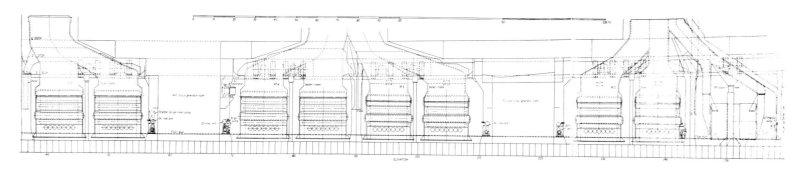

QUEEN MARY
LIVERPOOL

The Wakefield Mechanical Lubricator is employed on the R.M.S. "Queen Mary"

40
39
38
37
36

EACH OF THE FOUR PROPELLERS *on the* "QUEEN MARY" WEIGHS 35 TONS AND EACH ONE MEASURES 20 FEET FROM TIP TO TIP

THEY ARE SO DELICATELY BALANCED THAT THEY CAN BE TURNED WITH A TOUCH OF THE HAND

'In the bowels of the ship they are as yet only making ready for these colossal units of machinery. Men in dungarees, with electric lamps strapped to their heads, are crouched in dark corners, rigging what look like stupendous "Meccano" sets. Alone they work, in dank gloom, or in little clusters of twos and threes, making understanding signs to each other in the inferno of oxy-acetylene welding, which throws grotesque lilac shadows on the red-lead walls. Much of the work down here cannot be supervised all the time; the men proceed on their own, most of their actions depending upon their individual skill and integrity;.yet well and truly are these engine-rooms prepared for the vital forces soon to rest there. In one of the boiler-rooms – loftier and wider than many a country church – great girders rear up on either side, of the sort of girth you see when watching the building of a big departmental store...

'You can go even lower than the engine-rooms and stand on the double bottom of the ship that stretches throughout her length. Here you have over six feet of headroom. She is a ship within a ship, for she has an inner and outer skin, with over 160 water-tight compartments below the bulkhead deck. The space between the inner skin and the outer shell of the ship, in some places, is nearly 20 feet wide...

'You have of course never seen such boilers, such huge condensers – nobody has. There has never been constructed so gigantic a rudder for any vessel in maritime history. When finally in posi-

tion it will weigh nearly 150 tons – equivalent to the weight of 25 tramcars. Even these experts, not given to egotism, have to admit that this is the finest rudder ever designed, although the design is theirs. Another impression is, as it were, shot at you with the information that the total weight of the huge castings which form the shaft brackets, stern-post, rudder stock and frame approaches 600 tons. One of these castings alone, the rudder stock, weighs 90 tons. They have to cut a key-way in this rudder stock to a limit of 10,000th of an inch. The steering gear will weigh about 160 tons...

'They show you a 60-ton gear-wheel being adjusted "to a limit of half a thou" for grinding – a very difficult job which may take a week. The heavier the object, as they explain (seeing your stare of horror), the more difficult to adjust to a fine limit. Behind a cage in an isolated place they show you a gear-wheel 14 feet in diameter. Its teeth are being cut to a 1,000th of an inch of accuracy. It revolves, so slowly as to seem almost

Opposite page An advertisement placed by C C Wakefield & Co Ltd, supplier of the *Queen Mary's* oil lubrication pumps, in the commemorative issue of *The Shipbuilder*.

Above left The *Queen Mary's* four 35-ton manganese-bronze propellors each had four blades, measuring seven feet across. In this illustration from the 'Book of Comparisons' they are typically shown 'larger than life'. The caption boasts that they are so delicately balanced they can be turned with a touch of the hand.

Below One of the *Queen Mary's* propellers being inspected in dry dock at Southampton.

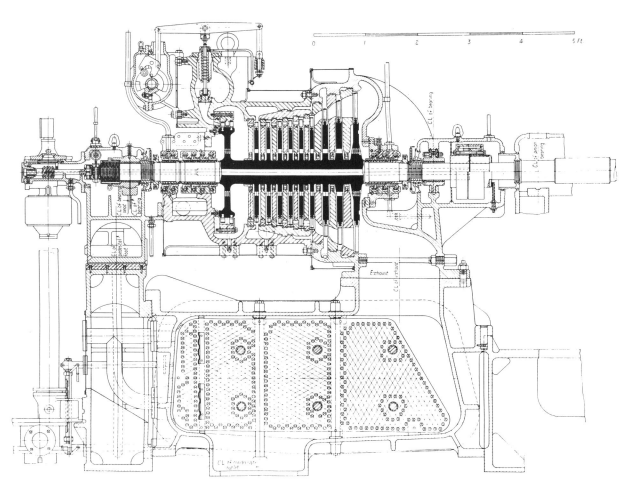

Right A longitudinal section through one of the *Queen Mary*'s electric-generator turbines. The power plant comprised seven such turbo-generators, each with an output of 1300 kw. Four of these sets supplied electric power for the ship's propulsion systems and three sets supplied the liner's hotel services. The hotel sets were located forward between numbers 1 and 2 boiler rooms. The main machinery sets were arranged in the after turbo-generator room between boiler rooms 4 and 5.

Below An illustration from the 'Book of Comparisons': the *Queen Mary*'s electrical energy was sufficient to meet the lighting and public service needs of a city of 150,000 people.

Opposite page An advertisement for Metrovick winches as supplied for the *Queen Mary* by Metropolitan Vickers Ltd of Manchester.

Overleaf The *Queen Mary*, still known only by her shipyard designation *534*, on the slipway ready for launching.

SEVEN TURBO-GENERATORS DELIVER NEARLY 10,000 KILOWATTS PER HOUR. THIS ELECTRICAL ENERGY IS SUFFICIENT TO MEET THE LIGHTING AND PUBLIC SERVICE NEEDS OF A CITY OF 150,000 PEOPLE OR SUCH CITIES AS BRIDGEPORT, CONN, TULSA, OKLAHOMA, DES MOINES, IOWA, SAN DIEGO, CALIFORNIA, SALT LAKE CITY, UTAH, JACKSONVILLE, FLORIDA OR SPOKANE, WASHINGTON.

motionless, ceaselessly for over two months on this machine. And there are five of these gear-wheels to cut, four and one spare...

'Some of the steel castings came to them with much anxiety and trouble. There was, for example, the unique railway journey of the stern frame (190 tons), the shaft-brackets, lower-main-rudder posts and the upper-stock, from the Darlington Forge Company. It is 20 miles only from Darlington to Haverton Hill Dock on the Tees, but the rail journey took six hours, during the quiescence of a weekend. It took them a week to place this extraordinary freight on the eight special steel trucks; every inch and every pound had to be meticulously calculated. Six hundred and twenty-five tons was the load of that crawling train, with inch clearances only under some of the bridges. During the last seven miles of the journey, the grotesque train had to run on the wrong set of metals, with some of its load overhanging the other "road" by 12 feet; wherefore the driver had to go forward on foot at each signal box and obtain permission in writing to proceed. But there was not a scratch or a hitch during rail and sea journey from the forge to the Clyde...

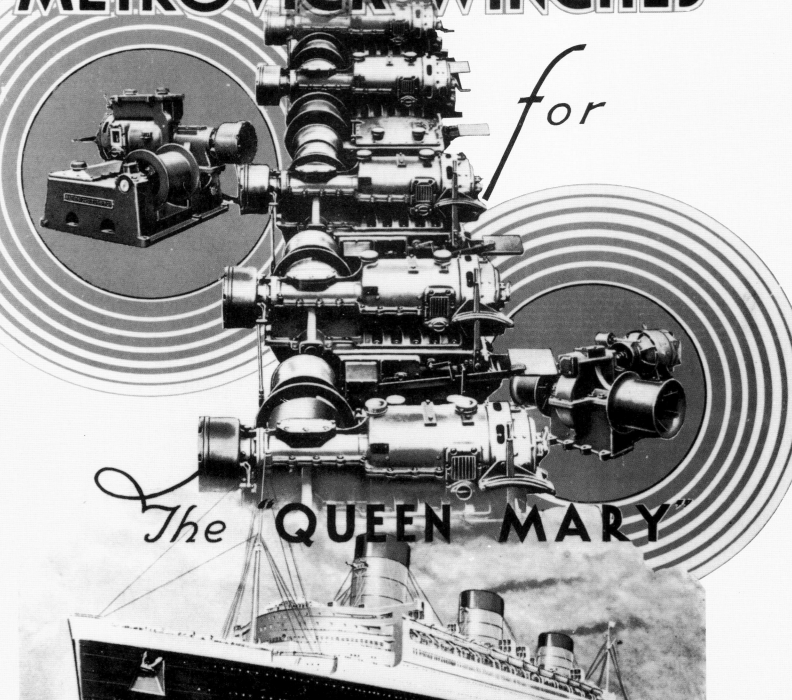

METROVICK WINCHES

for

The "QUEEN MARY"

METROPOLITAN Vickers

ELECTRICAL CO. LTD.
TRAFFORD PARK ••• MANCHESTER 17.

'The men who made these castings are the finest steelworkers in the world. Over 1,000 tons of molten steel were in the ladles for these castings. A ton and a half of screws and nails, and half a ton of glue were used in the construction of the wooden patterns for the moulds. Everything done by hand, and the greatest discrepancy before these mammoth castings reached their finished state was one-sixteenth of an inch...

'There are four manganese bronze propellers; each weighs 35 tons and is worth about £7,000. The propeller shafts are like great guns, only much longer. They have linings of lignum vitae; an inexperienced eye can see at once with what care each of the thousands of little wooden blocks has been laid. Is it not curious that lignum vitae acts as a lubricant when in contact with water, and yet as fuel on your fire at home it is unsurpassed?..

'The two great anchors, each weighing 16 tons, of special design, are the largest, naturally, that have ever been constructed for an ocean liner, and they will be recessed into the bows to obviate wind resistance; with 165 fathoms of cable (990 feet), weighing 145 tons, attached to each. Elaborate tests were made during the manufacture of these cables to ensure their strength. A three-link piece of chain was successfully subjected to a strain of nearly 700 tons. This exceeded official requirements by over 400 tons. Then they took separate links, haphazard (each has a diameter of $4\frac{1}{8}$ inches) and bent them double while cold. During this ordeal they showed no signs of strain...

'Writing of cable, the mind flicks for a moment to another kind of cable on board; the cable required to carry electric energy throughout the ship. There will be 4,000 miles of this. Visualize a length of cable stretching from New York to San Francisco, and nearly 800 miles beyond into the Pacific Ocean – and there you have it. That amount will be needed...

Above A detail from the cover of the booklet produced by Cunard to commemorate the launch of *534*.

Right Her Majesty Queen Mary steps forward to the microphone and prepares to send the giant liner down the slipway: 'I am happy to name this ship the *Queen Mary*. I wish success to her and all who sail in her.'

Opposite page His Majesty King George V and Queen Mary pause to greet the thousands of spectators at John Brown's Clydebank yard. Many sheltered under umbrellas against the rain that fell intermittently throughout the launch day.

Overleaf The giant hull thunders down the slipway.

The "Queen Mary" left her launching ways on **Tallene** (Reg'd) NOW IN GENERAL USE BY THE ADMIRALTY AND THE LEADING SHIPBUILDERS
Sole Makers
FERGUSON, SHAW & SONS, GLASGOW, C.4.
EST'D. 1843

'To glean a general impression of what happens to 40,000 tons of hand-wrought steelwork at the launch you must walk about underneath her keel in semi-darkness, and for quite a long time. You will appear to be in a tube tunnel with timber sides and a steel roof. You will not be able to see more than about 100 yards ahead of you either way, and the sunlight of a summer day will be almost entirely blotted out. Acres of tree-trunks stand at a slant against her steel – they felled four forests for the timber purposes of No *534*; and a quite uncountable number of massive wooden beams, piled upon each other, form her temporary bed. To penetrate herein with another man is almost instantly to lose him, for one baulk of timber is like unto another, and gloomy corners can be reckoned in hundreds...

'And "the wan water of the Clyde" has been prepared to receive her. For months one has seen the monotonous perambulation of the dredger buckets out in the stream; their high-pitched protestations drowned by a fiercer, more dynamic noise on shore. Five and a half acres of the river bank hereabouts have had to be removed to let her pass without impediment. The Clyde Trustees have contributed £80,000 that the river may be ready for her coming. Unusual arrangements

SHIP AT REST. DISTANCE TRAVELLED 1,196'
DRAFT ATA.P. 24'-1"
OBSERVED PATH OF AFTER CRADLE
POSI
IMMERSION

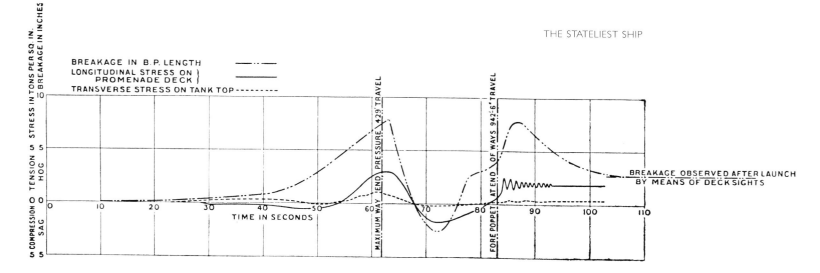

have been made in New York, comfortably to harbour her, and the world's biggest graving dock was dug out of the Southampton earth, expressly for her needs...

'We shall never know, categorically, the extent and scope of scientific thought that has been expended upon this tremendous project, because the men responsible for it all are by nature reserved, abhorring adulation, preferring infinitely to be left alone – that they may proceed unhampered, even further. Imagination tells us that there must have been great expectations that miraged into greater disappointments; perplexities that were but a spur; triumphs, minor and magnificent, that galvanized tired brains; calculations that cross-checked only to contradict; solutions that emerged suddenly to clarify gloom. But in the long end certainty...

'A few things, however, we do know, because reticence cannot hide them. We know – associate with the engineers behind the business even for one day in this yard and you become conscious of it – that every square foot of steel, every

pound of weight, every measurable quantity, capacity or function that forms part of the ship's structure, equipment or capability is there only because its quality has been superabundantly proved, and British craftsmen's brains and hands mobilized thereafter to set it in place.'

The day of the launch, 26 September 1934, was grey and wet, but the rain failed to dampen the enthusiasm of the more than 200,000 people who turned out for the event. Speculation about the name of the ship, which had still not been revealed, was rife, especially because the Cunard White Star Line had openly solicited names from the public. Responses, which ran the gamut from 'Queen Britannia' and 'Cunardia' to 'Gigantia' and 'Palatania', mostly all reflected the tradition begun with Cunard's first packet steamer *Britannia*, of using names that ended in 'ia' rather than the 'ic' preferred by the White Star Line. An apocryphal story, perpetuated by the daughter of Sir Ashley Sparke who was the chairman of the Cunard Line in America at the time, described how he, along with a small delegation from the company, were granted a royal audience to seek

Opposite page above An advertisement for Tallene, a slipway lubricant manufactured by Ferguson, Shaw & Sons of Glasgow.

Below A diagram prepared by the engineers at John Brown's yard, showing the *Queen Mary*'s actual performance during the launch procedure.

Above During the launch, four separate strain meters on the promenade deck recorded the stresses affecting the hull as it left the slipway. This diagram shows the readings obtained from one of these meters.

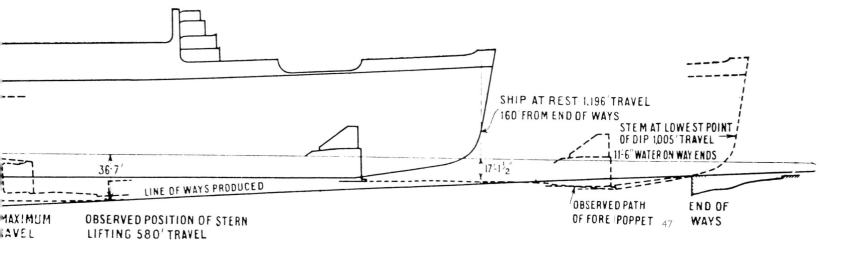

permission to use the name 'Queen Victoria'. As she has related, 'My father opened the conversation with His Majesty by saying ... that Cunard wished to name its new superliner, "after England's greatest queen". Queen Mary, who was with her husband on the occasion, smiled and said, "I would be delighted".' Company officials, however, refuted this story; and, indeed, the truth is much more prosaic. Cunard liners were popularly referred to as 'the queens of the North Atlantic', and board discussions then referred to building another two queens for the Atlantic run. Because of its charm and quirky verisimilitude, however, the myth of the misunderstood name continues, and perhaps the true reason why job number *534* was finally named the *Queen Mary* lies somewhere in between.

The multitudes who arrived at the Clydebank railway station opposite the gates of the John Brown shipyard, filled the long narrow deck between the berth where the ship had been laboriously pieced together, and the River Clyde, which had been newly dredged to a distance of 1,800 feet from the slipway, and widened to accommodate the length of the ship, as it slid into the water. The flat fields opposite, which look much the same today as they did then, also had viewing stands, which were hastily erected near the shore, to provide a more dramatic perspective on the event, and small boats out on the river carried celebrants who wanted an even closer look. From inside a glass enclosure which

Above Crowds thronged the banks of the Clyde opposite John Brown's yard, eager to see the new liner take to the water for the first time. Those nearest the river's edge got their feet wet as the *Queen Mary* sent a two-foot wave speeding in her wake as she left the slipway.

Opposite Tugs take charge of the world's largest hull and guide the *Queen Mary* to the fitting-out basin where she would spend the next 18 months having her machinery and interior fittings installed.

protected the royal couple from the rain, King George V made a speech that evoked the mood of hope, tempered with a painful awareness of the threat that had been posed by the Depression to this symbol of national pride:

'Today we come to the happy task of sending on her way the stateliest ship now in being. I thank all of those here and elsewhere whose efforts, however conspicuous or humble, have helped to build her, for three years her unaccomplished hull has laid in silence in the stocks. We know full well what misery a silent dockyard may spread among a seaport and with what courage that misery is endured. During those years when work upon her was suspended we grieved for what that suspension meant to thousands of our people. We rejoice that, with the help of my government, it has been possible to lift that cloud and complete this ship. Now, with the hope of better trade on both sides of the Atlantic, let me look forward to her playing a great part in the revival of international commerce. It has been the nation's will that she should be completed, and today we send her forth, no longer a number on the books, but a ship with a name, into the world, alive with beauty, energy and strength.'

Then, in a rare public appearance, Queen Mary cut the ribbon that would send a deliberately modest (and un-French) bottle of Australian champagne to smash against the hull and said, 'I am happy to name this ship the *Queen Mary*. I wish success to her and all who sail in her.' In the excitement of the moment, most people in the crowd missed the whispered question that followed, but those who tuned to the radio broadcast all over the country heard her turn to Lord Aberconway, chairman of John Brown and Company, and ask, 'Was that alright?'.

The speed with which the launch took place has been clocked variously at 65, 100 and 112 seconds in differing accounts, depending on the point at which the hull was felt to have stopped, and belies the builders' apprehension as they watched the event, since the short trip from the slipway

into the river subjected the vessel to critical bending stresses unlike any that it would experience at sea. These had given its engineers pause, and were the subject of extensive calculations beginning in the spring of 1930 as part of the original tender. They revolved around questions of declivity and camber in the ways and for the ship, considering that adequate space had to be provided beneath the launching way to allow workmen to have access to the hull. An early estimate of a launching weight of 40,000 tons was later reduced to 36,700 tons, including the weight of the cradle, and yet despite this reduction, it was still the heaviest mass of metal that John Brown's yard had ever dealt with. Unpredictable factors, for example, the possibility of high wind on launch day, led to precautions such as reinforcement of the end of the slipway, and the provision of 36 tons of anchors to offset slewing, once the hull was afloat. Careful records of the tides on the river between 1929 and 1933 were also commissioned, as well as a forecast of those for August and September, which indicated that with more than eight feet of water being available over the way ends on 26 September, it was the most favourable day for the launch. In fact, an exceptionally high tide on the day supplied three more feet of water than anticipated over the way ends.

The performance of the hull during the launch had been predicted by the ship's designers using an experimental model which proved accurate to a remarkable degree, even down to the distance it would travel after it hit the water, which, at 1,194 feet, was only two feet more than calculated; 2,350 tons of drag chains were used to slow the process down. The hull displaced so much water that it created a two-foot-high wave which was pushed over to the opposite river bank, washing into the spectator stands there. The precautions that the engineers had taken to prevent buckling of the hull, which included internal shoring by hundreds of tons of steel girders, and a decision to delay the cutting of openings in the superstructure until fitting-out after launch, in order to add stiffness to the shell, proved to be

Opposite Newly arrived in the fitting-out basin at John Brown's Clydebank yard, the *Queen Mary* awaits the installation of the immense power plant that would make her the fastest liner in the world.

wise, since films taken at the moment of impact showed that the pivoting point for structural purposes was almost 50 feet nearer to the stern than anticipated, due to the confining action of the river banks which the testing model had missed. As it was, the maximum 'hog' or upward deflection of the hull as it passed over the way ends was 7.9 inches, and the maximum sag was 2.6 inches, which was within the normal range, based on past experience.

After all the extensive preparations that had been made and the atmosphere of high excitement surrounding the event, the entire proceedings took barely 15 minutes to complete, from the moment that Queen Mary pushed the launch button to the second that the hull came to rest in the water. Tugs guided the ship into the fitting-out basin located upriver from the slipway, where it would spend the next 20 months being converted from an empty shell into the 'stateliest ship' that George V had anticipated. While nearly 1,000 tons of Burma teak had been cut and installed as decking, ladders and handrails before the ship slid down the ways into the water (difficult to replicate today, given the environmental consciousness that now prevails), everything else required to transform it into a functioning ocean-going vessel still remained to be done.

One of the first tasks was to prepare the empty hull to accept the heart of what was to become known as 'the greatest power plant afloat'. The critical components of that power plant were the turbines, which, along with the boilers that would feed them, were produced by the John Brown Company, at the same Clydebank facility where the hull was built. Each of the four turbine groupings, corresponding directly to the four propellers used to drive the ship, consisted of one high-pressure, two intermediate-pressure and one low-pressure turbine working in series, with each turbine driving a separate pinion connected to the main propeller gear-wheel. The turbines were made up of an intricate array of blades individually fitted into grooves in the rotors which drove them. Hundreds of separate

stainless steel blades were fixed in place by brazing, and finally secured by locking strips, positioned by hand. When all of the blades were in place, each rotor was individually balanced to ensure that no vibration would occur. The enormous size of the turbines required the manufacture of special balancing machinery to adjust them, capable of turning their 42-ton cylinders.

The steam required to turn these four massive turbine groupings, and ultimately the propellers themselves, which would drive the Queen Mary through the water at record speeds was generated in five separate boiler rooms; one room was allocated to each of the four turbine groupings, and a fifth acted as an auxiliary, back-up unit. In each of the four main, on-line compartments, six water-tube boilers fitted with superheaters and air-heaters were built for John Brown by Yarrow and Company of Scotstown, Glasgow. Each of these boilers was of the double-flow variety, built to operate at a pressure of 400 pounds per square inch, and an average temperature of 700 degrees fahrenheit. Each boiler included one steam-, three water- and one superheater-drum with sufficient space provided for longitudinal expansion. All five drums were positioned around a central, oil-fired furnace. Each boiler was entirely sheathed in a steel casing, with a furnace lined with fire-brick, and the whole assembly wrapped in a second, outer shell, allowing air to circulate around it and keep it cool. Each day that a boiler was in operation, it required 150,000 gallons of purified, softened water, which was carefully monitored to ensure that mineral deposits would not clog the 6,500 boiler tubes. In all 8,300 tons of oil, stored in bunkers occupying a deep-zone of the ship's perimeter section, from amidships to stern, at F, G and H deck levels, was pumped into settling tanks as needed, where it was preheated, filtered and then heated again until it reached the proper consistency to be sprayed through the 168 nozzles serving the four furnaces, where the water was superheated to steam. Blower fans were used to ensure efficient combustion, and these created such a cyclonic force within the boiler rooms that each required an

Above A small army of shipyard workers streams down the gangways at the end of the working day. Hundreds of men were employed at the John Brown yard to ensure that fitting out was completed on time.

air-lock to equalize the pressure for the ship's engineers working inside.

In the hyperbole-laden journalistic style somewhat typical of the decade in which the *Queen Mary* was launched, one popular magazine managed to approximate the hidden, below-deck drama in the engine-room in the following description, using similes that make the engineering achievement more comprehensible: 'The steam from the boilers,' it begins, 'is piped to the turbines, where its tremendous, bursting energy is harnessed to the task of turning four gear wheels 14 feet in diameter. The harness is called

a turbine. It operates like a hermetically-sealed windmill, only in place of wind there is steam blasting out of flared nozzles, and instead of big vanes there are tiny blades – each tested and fitted by hand. Pounding madly from the boilers the steam charges into the high-pressure turbine, loses part of its energy in turning the blades, passes somewhat chastened to the second, third and fourth turbines, which work at successively lower pressures until, thoroughly tamed, the steam collapses into condensers that return it as water to the boilers. Meanwhile, in its wild spree, the steam has done its work. It has whirled the tiny windmill blades at 3,600 revolutions per

Above In the engine-room, an engineer confirms instructions from the bridge on one of the *Queen Mary*'s telegraphs.

Below An illustration from the 'Book of Comparisons': the main engines of the *Queen Mary* generated approximately 200,000 horse power, or equal to that of 50 passenger locomotives.

minute normal speed. Each pinion of the four turbines is geared to the big 14-foot gear wheel by double-helical teeth accurate to one-half of one thousandth of an inch. So the big wheel, 15 times greater than the pinions in circumference, turns over 240 times a minute. From this gear wheel a hollow steel shaft 27 ³⁄₈ inches in diameter extends aft, penetrates the stern of the hull and holds at its outboard end a 35-ton propeller, nearly 20 feet in diameter. The propeller and its three mates at the ends of the other tail shafts beat the water with such force as to set up an ear-splitting din within the hull, warp the blades perceptibly out of line, and push RMS *Queen Mary*, with 2,000 passengers, across the sea in four days – faster than any other liner afloat.'

None of the publicity photographs taken of the miscellaneous pieces of machinery amassed for assembly during fit-out convey the superhuman scale of this enterprise quite as effectively as those of the propellers, which were the ultimate recipients of the power generated by oil furnaces, steam boilers and turbines combined. The favoured backdrop of hastily assembled groups of workmen who were placed in front of them to heighten the effect of their size, the 35-ton propellers – the heaviest cast at the time – provided a symbol that was more familiar to the general public than a main-reduction-gear-wheel or a port-inner-main-condenser, and these four manganese-bronze masterpieces, produced in Deptford and Millwall, were frequently singled out for their share of superlatives.

In addition to the main propelling machinery of boilers, condensers, turbines, shafts and screws, and as well as the water-softening plant, oil bunkers and settling tanks that accompanied them, the electrical system was another complex and vital component of the fit-out process, with an equally impressive set of superlatives of its own. Having made the decision to rely upon electrically-driven auxiliary machinery to a greater extent than on any other British passenger ship, the designers of the *Queen Mary* equipped it with seven 1,300 kilowatt turbo generators, with four

of these allocated for the auxiliary services required in propulsion, and three designated for the ship's 'hotel' services. The extensive switchboards required for each group, located forward between boiler rooms one and two, and aft between boiler rooms four and five respectively, were placed on long raised metal platforms directly above their corresponding generators. These two supply-switchboards, when finally installed, presented a dizzying display of electrical power, with a panel 37 feet long servicing the 'hotel' and 46 feet long running along the main machinery room. Every precaution was taken to ensure an uninterrupted supply of current and to prevent fire. Specially-designed, instantaneous-overload relays, intended to operate at a predetermined load and trip secondary feeder-circuits were fitted to each of the turbo generators, to carry a certain portion of their load in an emergency situation, thus preventing an overload on the other generators if one should shut down. The compact, efficient arrangement of each of the extensive machinery switchboards belies the fact that the total lengths of cable fitted throughout the ship, if fully extended, would run for 735 miles, and the 9,100 kilowatts of power that it carried would have been sufficient for the electrical needs of a town with a population of 100,000. The complexity of the system, when viewed in this way, gives increased credence to

Below A poster by Tom Gentleman for the Shell Oil Company, 1935: 'RMS *Queen Mary* uses Shell Lubricating Oil exclusively for the generator turbines.'

R.M.S. "Queen Mary" uses

SHELL LUBRICATING OIL
EXCLUSIVELY FOR THE GENERATOR TURBINES

Top left An advertisement for 'Speedwell' wire ropes as selected for the *Queen Mary*'s lifeboats.

Top right The sun deck promenade, port side. The lifeboats on their davits form a protective canopy, through which light is filtered, throwing deep shadows on the deck below.

Above Detail of a lifeboat rudder and propeller.

Right An illustration from the 'Book of Comparisons': each one of the lifeboats could accommodate 145 people.

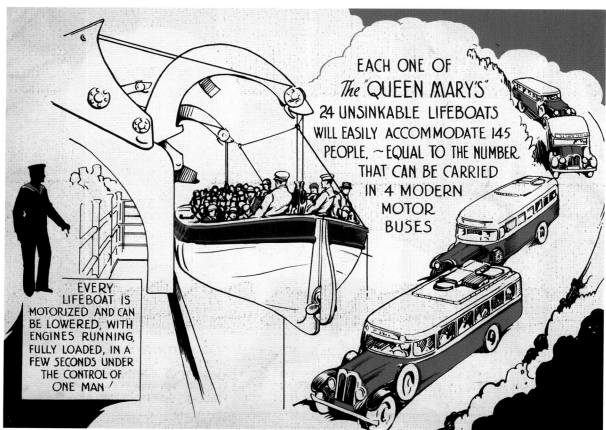

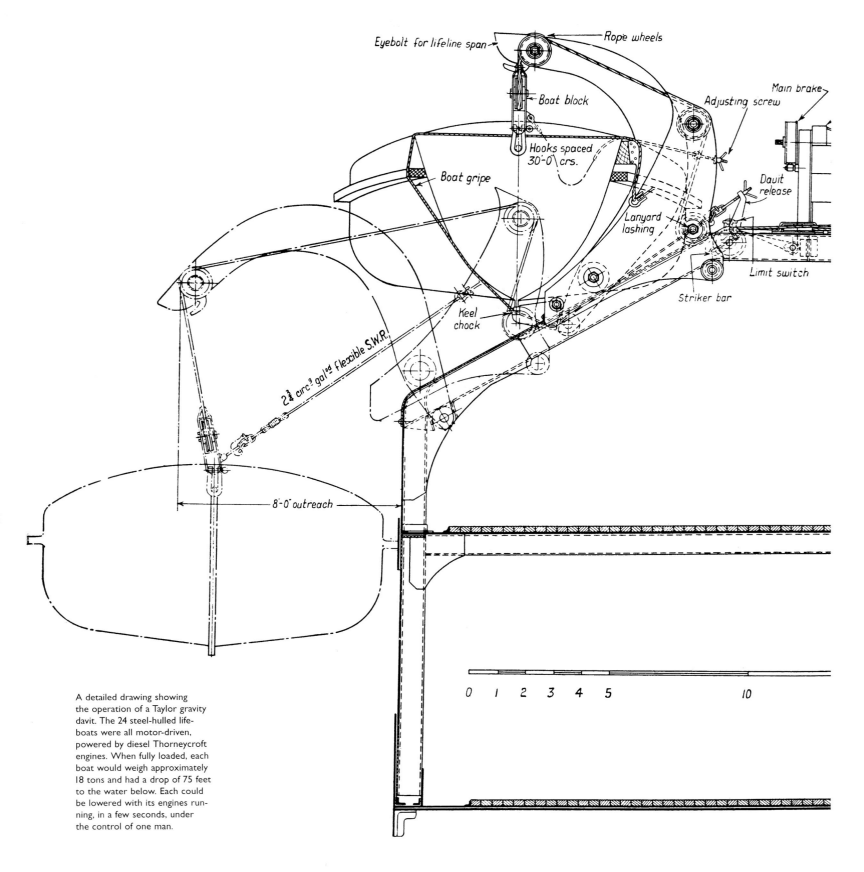

Eyebolt for lifeline span

Rope wheels

Boat block

Hooks spaced 30'-0" crs.

Main brake

Adjusting screw

Davit release

Boat gripe

Lanyard lashing

Limit switch

Striker bar

Keel chock

2¾ circ⁵ gal⁶ flexible S.W.R.

8'-0" outreach

0 1 2 3 4 5   10

A detailed drawing showing the operation of a Taylor gravity davit. The 24 steel-hulled lifeboats were all motor-driven, powered by diesel Thorneycroft engines. When fully loaded, each boat would weigh approximately 18 tons and had a drop of 75 feet to the water below. Each could be lowered with its engines running, in a few seconds, under the control of one man.

the notion that this was not merely a ship, but a veritable city afloat.

Of all the myriad additions made to the *Queen Mary* during the long fitting-out process, there were several in particular which, while extremely pragmatic, helped to establish her singular identity. The lifeboats, for example, were required by the Board of Trade, which had imposed extremely stringent conditions ever since the sinking of the *Titanic* in 1912, in which a disproportionate loss of life was directly attributable to both a shortage of lifeboats and the inefficient use of those that existed. In that instance, a new type of electrically-driven davit had been installed to lower the boats. The crew, however, had not been instructed how to use it and, in lowering the boats by hand, hung many of the precious few craft that were available up on the lines. No drills were held, and because of the poorly-supervised loading of the boats, many of them were lowered half empty.

The *Queen Mary* carried ample lifeboats, 24 in all, cradled in Taylor gravity davits. These consis-

ted of sloping trackways, on which the hook-like mechanisms from which the boats were hung, were designed to run. While the descent was controlled by winches, it relied on gravity once the davits were released. The design was a novel one in that each cradle consisted of an arm and a carriage which were connected by a hinge. After the cradle was released and moved down the track, the arm swung outboard, automatically positioning the boat into the proper alignment for lowering. As it reached the bottom of the cradle, the lower part of the arm slowed down, thus avoiding sudden impact and any damage to each boat. Each track was made of two rolled-steel channels with webs turned outwards to carry the wheels of the carriage which ran on the flanges. The tracks were protected from ice formation by tightly-stretched flexible guards, also intended to improve the appearance of the assembly and prevent any grease from falling on to the deck below. The final effect of these repetitive, angular tracks that spanned both sides of the sun deck was that of a rhythmic, partially open canopy, which provided little sense of the emergency service that it served, since the boats above were only partially visible to those walking beneath. The light streaming through the broad steel supports gave the long narrow runs of the port and starboard side of the sun deck a singular

Opposite page The last section of the after funnel sits on the quayside at John Brown's yard awaiting installation.

Above left A view of the midships funnel taken by Madame Yevonde, a noted society photographer who was commissioned to capture the *Queen Mary* on precious colour film as the finishing touches were made prior to her maiden voyage.

Below An illustration from the 'Book of Comparisons': three locomotives placed abreast could pass through the *Queen Mary*'s forward funnel.

The FORWARD FUNNEL *of the* "QUEEN MARY" IS 70 FEET IN HEIGHT FROM THE BOAT DECK. (A FOOT HIGHER THAN THE EGYPTIAN OBELISK, IN CENTRAL PARK, NEW YORK CITY) THE DIAMETER OF EACH FUNNEL IS 30 FEET AND WOULD PERMIT 3 MODERN LOCOMOTIVES, PLACED ABREAST, TO PASS THROUGH, OR TO ENCLOSE THE HULL OF THE FIRST CUNARDER, THE "BRITANNIA."

appeal, while the promenade deck, directly below, seemed somewhat claustrophobic in comparison.

As on all passenger liners, lifeboat drills were always mandatory during the first full day of every crossing on the *Queen Mary*. The lifeboats, at 12 feet wide by 36 feet long, were the largest ever to be carried in davits at the time they were installed. Steel-hulled and motor-driven by 18 bhp two-cylinder diesel engines that made them capable of speeds of up to six knots, they were a far cry from those carried on the *Titanic* and were sturdy, dependable craft in their own right, each capable of carrying 145 people, more than were transported by the first Cunard liner *Britannia*.

In addition to the array of lifeboats, the whistles for signalling, which similarly serve a practical function, also added to the *Queen Mary*'s distinctive identity. They were personalized by the press at the time of the maiden voyage as

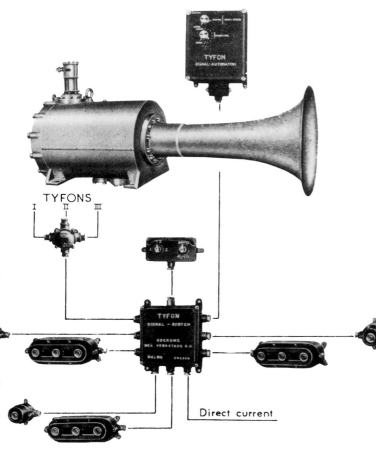

Top right A diagrammatic representation of one of the *Queen Mary*'s three Tyfon whistles which were operated electrically from a control panel on the bridge.

Right A page from the 'Book of Comparisons': 'the larynx of the Queen' could emit a lower base A note so powerful that it could be heard at a distance of at least ten miles.

Opposite page Workmen secure one of the Tyfon whistles on the forward funnel. Each whistle weighed approximately one ton and was seven feet long.

Above The *Queen Mary* at her fitting-out berth in John Brown's yard. Smoke pouring from the forward funnel indicates that the boilers are being fired for the first time. Against the backdrop of this machine-age drama, 1930's agricultural life on Clydebank seems stuck in the pattern of the previous century.

Opposite page An aerial view of the *Queen Mary* at John Brown's yard taken before the fitting of the after funnel; the funnel midships is also missing its distinctive black top.

Overleaf left Painters at John Brown's yard picking out the letters of *Queen Mary*'s name and marking the top-most line of the black section of the hull.

Overleaf right The *Queen Mary* rests in the King George V Graving dock in Southampton prior to making her maiden voyage.

'the larynx of the Queen'. Even the stolidly factual *Shipbuilder*, in its special issue dedicated to the new liner, alluded to the special quality of their tone, by saying that: 'the sound signals emitted by larger passenger vessels should be sufficiently distinctive to indicate the size of the vessel of origin – if not, indeed, to identify it – while at the same time they must not be of harsh or strident quality likely to irritate or disturb the passengers. These conditions are most adequately met by signalling apparatus giving a note of very low pitch, to secure which whistles of large dimensions are essential. The *Queen Mary* is equipped with three Tyfon whistles, two of which are mounted on the forward funnel, the third being fitted to the middle funnel. Designed to give a deep base A note of frequency 60 per second, they are operated by steam at a pressure of about 140 pounds

per square inch. Some idea of the enormous size of these Tyfon whistles may be given by the fact that each weighs one ton, with a horn that is six feet seven inches long, while the diameter of the diaphragm is 22 1/2 inches.'

The sleek ship that left the fitting-out basin in April 1936 looked quite different from the empty grey hull that had swept down the launching slipways 19 months previously. Sea trials off the Isle of Arran, which were to follow, would determine the extent to which all of the design decisions, just implemented, had been successful, and a critical phase in the *Queen Mary's* career was soon to begin. On 24 March she left the Firth of Clyde for the open sea, bound for Southampton from where she would sail on her maiden voyage to New York.

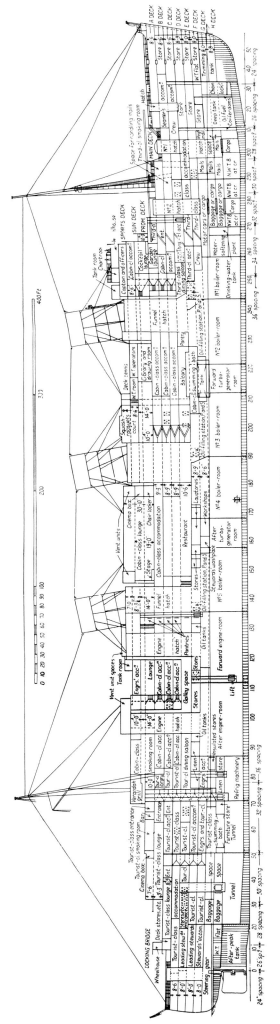

INBOARD ELEVATION OF THE QUEEN MARY

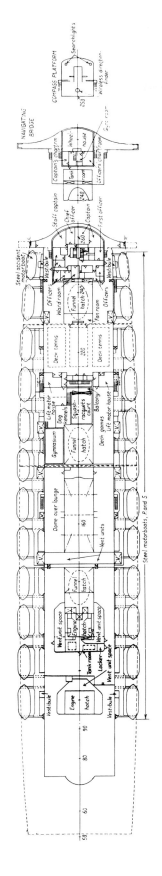

SPORTS DECK

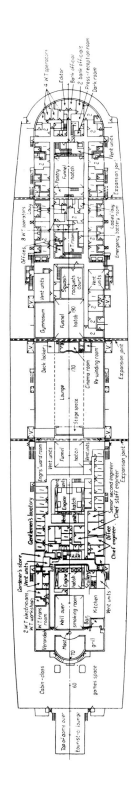

SUN DECK

A DECK

68 cinema film store
69 A deck tourist lounge
70 tourist entrance, staircase, lifts
71 suites and bedroom accommodation
72 staircase and lifts
73 staterooms and suites
74 staircase and lifts
75 switch room
76,77 staterooms and suites
78 staircase and lifts
79 purser's office
80 staterooms and suites
81 forward staircase and lifts
82 third-class hairdresser's
83 third-class entrance
84 third-class smoking room
85 fore hatch
86 rope store
87 forecastle and anchor capstan

B DECK

88 crew
89 suites and bedroom accommodation
90 staircase and lifts
91 suites and bedroom accommodation
92 hairdresser's
93 staircase and lifts
94 suites and bedrooms
95 staircase and lifts
96, 97 staterooms and suites
98 staircase and lifts
99 hairdresser's and beauty parlour
100 staterooms and suites
101 forward staircase and lifts
102 third-class children's playroom
103 third-class lounge
104 mail-handling space
105 capstan gear
106 crew

C DECK

107 crew
108 capstan space
109 bedroom accommodation
110 staircase and lifts
111 suites and bedroom accommodation
112 staircase and lifts
113 tourist dining saloon
114 baker's shop
115 vegetable-preparing room
116 kitchens
117 grill
118 china pantry
119 bar
120 private dining rooms
121 restaurant
122 private dining rooms
123 foyer
124 third-class dining room
125 third-class entrance
126 third-class accommodation
127 capstan gear and crew's space

D DECK

128 crew
129 suites and bedroom accommodation
130 baggage lift well
131 suites and bedroom accommodation
132 tourist staircase and lifts
133 suites and bedroom accommodation
134 ales and stout
135 stores entrance
136 ice-cream, butter and milk
137 fruit-ripening room
138 fruit stores
139 vegetable and salad room
140 fresh and frozen fish
141 butcher's shop and meat store
142 poultry, game, etc
143 bacon and eggs
144 grocery store
145 hospital
146 dispensary
147 printers' shop
148 third-class accommodation
149 oil-filling station
150 third-class accommodation
151 swimming pool dressing room
152 swimming pool
153 kosher kitchen
154 third-class kitchens
155 third-class accommodation
156 crew

SPORTS DECK

1 main mast
2–7 ventilators
8 staircase
9 space for deck sports, promenade and deck-tennis courts
10, 11 tank room
12 directional aerials
13 semaphores
14 searchlights
15 chart room
16 wheel-house and bridge
17 captain's and officers' quarters

SUN DECK

18 verandah grill
19 engineer officers' accommodation
20 engineers' ward room
21 cinema projection room
22 gymnasium
23 squash rackets court
24 lift gear
25 wireless receiving room
26 staterooms and suites
27 forward staircase and lifts
28 staterooms and suites

PROMENADE DECK

29 cinema projection room
30 tourist smoking room
31 pantry
32 tourist entrance
33 smoking room
34 pantry
35 after end of long gallery
36 staircase and lifts
37 ballroom
38 starboard gallery
39 pantry
40 stage of lounge
41 lounge
42 chair stowage
43 writing rooms
44 entrance
45 main hall and shopping centre
46 drawing room
47 altar
48 children's playroom
49 forward staircase and lifts
50 cocktail bar and observation lounge
51 promenade

MAIN DECK

52 docking bridge
53 tourist lounge
54 tourist staircase and lifts
55 tourist writing room and library
56 staterooms and suites
57 staircase and lifts
58 store room
59 staterooms and suites
60 main staircase and lifts
61 furniture stores
62 staterooms and suites
63 forward staircase and lifts
64 third-class garden lounge
65 cargo hatch
66 fore mast
67 crow's nest

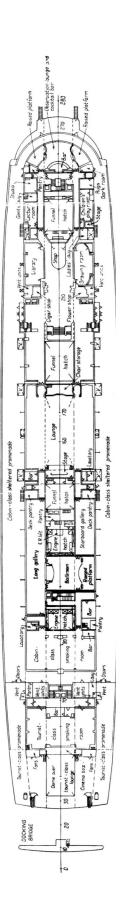

PROMENADE DECK

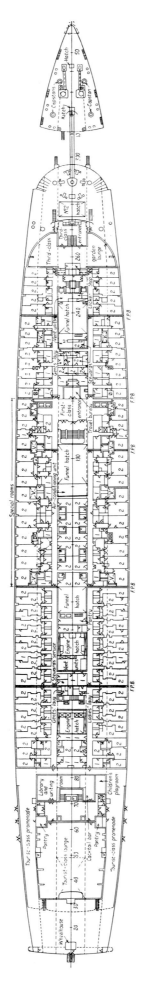

MAIN DECK

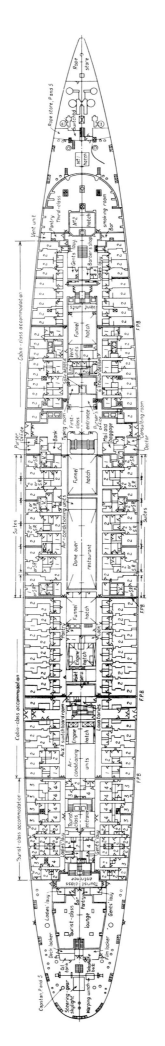

A DECK

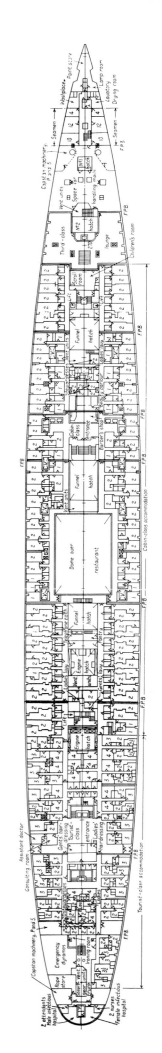

B DECK

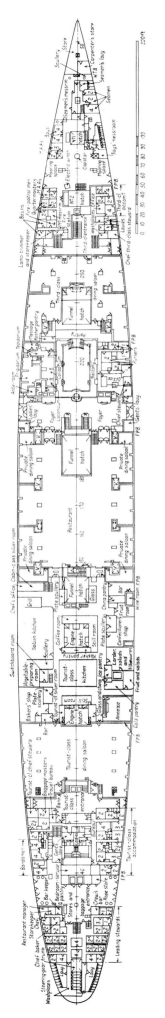

C DECK

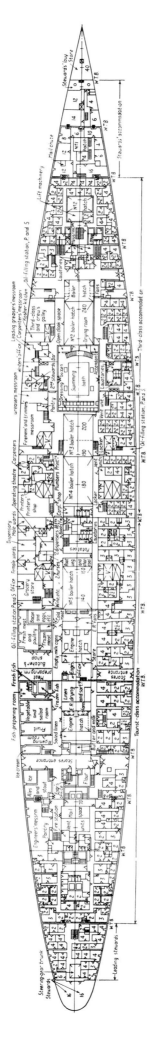

D DECK

E DECK

14

16

28

SPORTS DECK

50

SUN DECK

51

64

PROMENADE DECK
65

66

67

MAIN DECK

82   83   84   85   86   87

"A" DECK

QUEEN MARY

102   103   104   105   106

"B" DECK

24   125   126   127

"C" DECK

155   156

"D" DECK

162   163   164   165

"E" DECK

197

172   173

"F" DECK

198   199   179

"G" DECK   178   201

"H" DECK   200

202   202

203

GH TAVIS

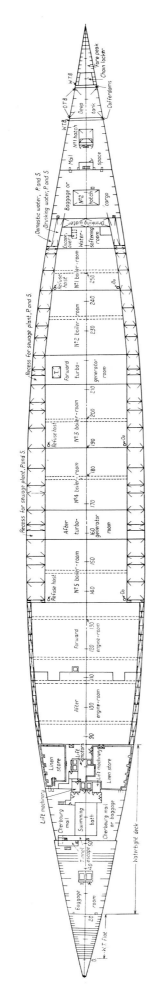

F DECK

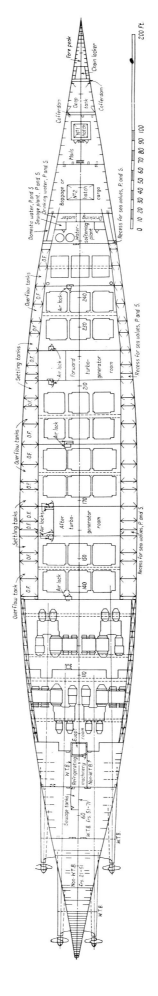

G DECK

H DECK

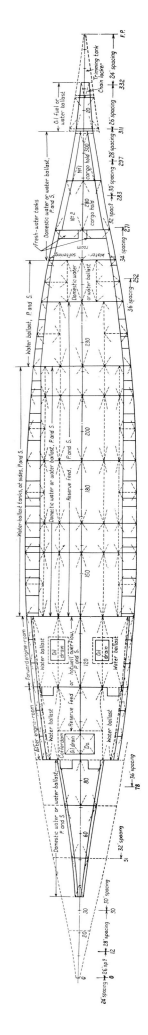

TANK TOP

Newly completed, the *Queen Mary* undergoes sea trials off the Isle of Arran in April 1936. In this photograph the ship can be seen making a high-speed turn to port, one of the many manœuvres designed to test her stability and performance at sea.

Early in the morning of Monday 25 May 1936, King Edward VIII who, as the Duke of Windsor

An ingenious deck-map model of the *Queen Mary*, an invaluable guide to the cavernous interior of the ship.

would become so intimately associated with the style of the *Queen Mary*, arrived at Southampton with a royal party that included Queen

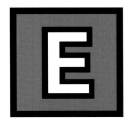

Mary herself, who had not seen her namesake since the launch two years before. The party also included the Duke and Duchess of York, and their daughter Princess Elizabeth. The King, who had shown

A marble plaque of Her Majesty Queen Mary; carved by Lady Hilton Young it was located at the head of the main cabin-class staircase.

a consistent interest in the liner's construction, was given a stem-to-stern tour of the ship which lasted most of the day.

The epitome of elegance and luxury, the *Queen Mary* represented a glamorous and seductive way of life.

Opposite Bell boys assembled for a group photograph on the sports deck under the watchful eye of the chief steward.

The King, wearing a linen suit and jaunty straw hat, flew ahead of the royal party, landing at Atlantic Park on the outskirts of Southampton, and proceeded by car to the ship shortly before the royal train steamed into the docks from Waterloo. It was the King's fourth visit to the ship and his second in three months; his previous tour had taken place on 5 March as the ship prepared to leave Clydebank for its sea trials.

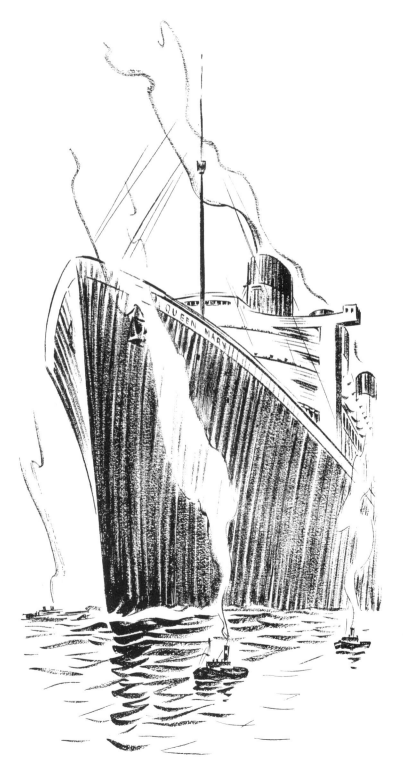

On that occasion King Edward had covered a good eight and a half miles on foot, guided by Donald Skiffington, John Brown's shipyard manager and the man who had driven the first rivet in the hull two years earlier. The King climbed ladders, descended in lifts, questioned the shipyard workers about their tasks and after lunching with officials of the company went straight from the luxury of the liner to examine for himself some of the worst slum housing in the country which lay almost beneath its shadow. In contrast, at Southampton the royal party was received on the quayside by Sir Alfred Bates, chairman of the Cunard White Star Line, and at the head of the gangway by Commodore Sir Edgar Britten, the *Queen Mary*'s first commander. *The Times* in a pre-visit report noted that:

'A special suite, which will be decorated with sweet peas, carnations, roses and lilies of the valley, has been reserved for the use of the Queen, who is not expected to carry out the full inspection of the ship. The King and his two brothers have intimated a special desire to see the engines of the ship, which is expected to create a speed record, but the ladies of the party are likely to be more interested in the "homely" arrangements of the vessel. The Queen particularly desires to see the kitchen, and Princess Elizabeth is to make a special tour of the children's playroom, in which there are rare fishes, which have cost many pounds each. The royal party will lunch on board in the dining saloon, and the floral decorations will be in shades of soft pink to harmonise with the general scheme of furnishings. The ship's gardener, Mr A Davis, has had a busy time decorating the liner. Between 700 and 800 flowering plants, ferns and ornamental shrubs are distributed throughout the public rooms, and many very rare flowers add to the beauty of the ship. It has been decided that all work shall cease on the vessel during the period of the royal visit. There are about 400 men, apart from the ship's company, still engaged in rounding off numerous jobs, but they will be sent ashore shortly after ten o'clock on Monday morning, and only key men and officials will be allowed on the ship.'

An early Cunard poster exhorting tourists to visit 'America this year by RMS *Queen Mary*'. The tourist trade was of vital importance to Cunard and the other transatlantic shipping lines, replacing the pre-World War I immigrant trade as a significant source of income. The *Queen Mary* was one of the first Atlantic liners to have its second-class accommodation designated as 'tourist' in recognition of this changing trend.

the mechanized ideal of modernism, Art Deco thrived on handcraftsmanship, painstakingly implemented by artisans who delighted in the juxtaposition of elegant materials. After a name change to 'Moderne', it was officially adopted by the Roosevelt administration as a Federal style, and promoted in exhibitions in Paris in 1937 and New York in 1939. As in America, particularly in Los Angeles, London's cinemas and hotels of the period provide especially good examples of the genre.

The penchant for combining exotic materials, used by the best-known designers in all media, was perfectly reflected in the design philosophy of the *Queen Mary* where the theme of rare and luxurious materials led to its celebration as 'the ship of beautiful woods'. Specific vignettes throughout the ship echoed common themes in the style, of mythology, animals and natural settings, abstracted into pure form. Art Deco furniture designers, for example, relied heavily on ebony,

The new ship that *The Times* correspondent depicted was an Art Deco masterpiece, every inch the stylistic product of the age. As a style, Art Deco contrasted with Art Nouveau, to which it is frequently compared; instead of making an opposing commentary on the products and processes of the industrial age, it embraced and glorified them. Rather than being related to natural antecedents, forms were explored for their own sake; these were typically flatter, sleeker, more sensuous and representative of speed than their Art Nouveau antecedents. Art Deco designers used rare materials to express these ideas in combinations and inlays that accentuated their exotic character. The Art Deco style swept all areas of artistic endeavour in Europe between the time of the *Exposition des Arts Décoratifs* in Paris in 1925 and the beginning of World War II. The great French liners of the period, the *Ile de France* and the *Normandie*, were among the earliest maritime Art Deco exemplars. In the United States the style surfaced first in skyscraper design, flowering in the *Queen Mary*'s land-bound contemporary, the Chrysler Building in New York City in the early 1930s. The Chrysler's faceted stainless steel spire, detailed with characteristic chevron motifs, still dominates the skyline in a city in which the impetus for ever-taller buildings continues to break the record it set when it was built. Distinctly different from

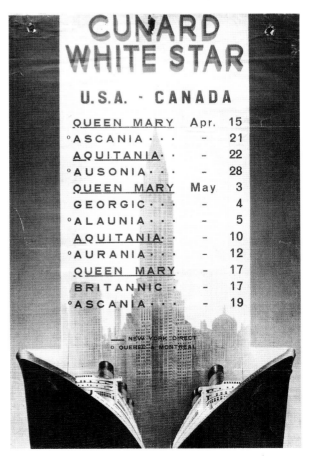

Opposite page An early view of the Chrysler Building in midtown Manhattan. Designed by William Van Alen, and completed in 1930, it is one of the world's great Art Deco masterpieces, exemplifying the stylistic age in which the *Queen Mary* was conceived. At 1,048 feet overall, it is as high at the base of its needle-like spire as the *Queen Mary* is long, and was briefly the tallest building in the world before being overtaken by the Empire State Building in 1931.

Above left The Chrysler Building's exuberant stainless-steel cap is illuminated at night, and appears to telescope upwards, heightening the building's vertical thrust.

Left A poster from the late 1930s advertising Cunard's weekly schedule of sailings to the United States and Canada. The liners illustrated against the backdrop of the Chrysler Building are the *Queen Mary* (left) and the *Queen Elizabeth*, but this two-ship service would not become a reality until after World War II. In the meantime, the *Queen Mary* alternated with the *Aquitania* and the *Berengaria* on the run to New York.

Above Art Deco elevator doors in the Chrysler Building. *Queen Mary*'s marquetry was every bit as accomplished although more modest in expression.

Below left An illustration from the 'Book of Comparisons' showing the *Queen Mary* alongside the Empire State Building.

Below right The Empire State Building, by Shreve Lamb & Harmon, was completed in 1931.

jacaranda, zebra wood and calamander, combined with veneers of mahogany, violetwood, sycamore, amarath and amboyna, as well as maple and ash burls. These were typically interposed with ivory, metals, shagreen and lacquer to convey a feeling of richness and sensuality. No British ship before or since has represented such a dedicated and singular commitment to an aesthetic philosophy, identifying it so clearly with the era in which it was built.

If we imagine we are accompanying the royal party, it will allow us a preview of the brand new vessel, prior to any passengers having been aboard. After entering across a long, carpeted gangway the royal party would have been given a second reception in the spacious foyer on A deck, where passengers would later have been met by a small army of pursers, stewards and porters, eager to assist them in checking the location of, and finding their cabins. On sailing days, this area would be a frenzy of activity. As described by one veteran of many crossings:

'There was always the awesome first sight of the ship's prow, like a giant knife blade, in the water. At the pier a messy commotion of longshoremen hauled bags from taxis and cars to a moving ramp, while passengers and bewildered visitors tottered under *Bon Voyage* baskets up their separate canvas-sided gang planks.' These separate entrances, of course, were related to the three classes of the ship, newly designated on the *Queen Mary* by the Cunard Line as cabin, tourist and third class, following the lead given by the *Normandie* the year before. Name changes such as this and the loss of 'first class', which eventually led all other companies involved in transport across the North Atlantic to adopt the name 'cabin ships', have more recently been attempted by airlines for the same reason, in the hope that passengers, when restricted by budget to the narrow cheaper seats 'down the back', will feel less resentful of those more fortunate souls in first and 'club class' in front, if they are designated as 'world travellers' rather than 'economy class'.

IF THE "QUEEN MARY" WERE PLACED IN FIFTH AVENUE

WITH ITS STERN AGAINST THE SIDE *of the* EMPIRE STATE BUILDING *at* 34ᵗʰ STREET, ITS LENGTH WOULD EXTEND ALMOST TO 38ᵗʰ STREET

English and American exemplars of an Art Deco age. *Clockwise from top left* The entrance lobby of 275 Madison Avenue, New York; a bathroom in the executive suite of the Chanin Building, New York, by Jacques Delamarre, 1929; Peter Jones Department Store, London, by W Crabtree, 1936–38; and Broadcasting House, London, by Val Myers and Watson-Hart, 1931.

65 PULLMAN SLEEPERS WOULD BE NEEDED TO MOVE THE 2075 PASSENGERS WHICH THE "QUEEN MARY" CAN CARRY ON ONE TRIP. ~ 15 COACHES WOULD BE NEEDED TO MOVE THE CREW, ~ COMPARED TO

The 200 PEOPLE THAT WERE PASSENGERS AND CREW ON THE FIRST CUNARDER "BRITANNIA"

Boarding the *Queen Mary*'s 2,000 potential cabin, tourist and third-class passengers on sailing days was a logistical feat in itself. In this page from the 'Book of Comparisons', Cunard boasted that 65 Pullman sleepers would be needed to transport the liner's full complement of passengers, with another 15 required for the crew.

In the *Queen Mary*, great efforts were made to avoid such distinctions, in design, accommodation and service. Press promotions constantly referred to the fact that third class, on this ship, was the equivalent of first class elsewhere, all in an effort to sell more tickets. The cabin-class entrance, corresponding to the foyer on A deck, was located near the stairs and lifts, rising vertically adjacent to the second of the three funnels, and serving staterooms on the sun and main decks. The tourist-class entrance located near the stern, was also next to a stair and lift tower, corresponding to the third funnel, while third-class passengers entered far below the bridge, with their vertical circulation related to the first funnel.

Returning to the royal tour beginning at the A deck foyer, the lift, leaving from there, terminated on the sports deck which served as the roof of the ship in the cabin-class section. At 60 feet above the water line it was the highest passenger deck on the ship, and was to become the favourite venue for tennis, shuffleboard and quoits addicts, as well as for those wishing to visit their pets in the kennels near the lift tower. This deck is separated from the wheelhouse and bridge by the first of the *Queen Mary*'s three massive funnels, which was raised higher than the others to create a rakish triangular line from stem to stern. These funnels have the characteristic orange-red body and black rim that have become a symbol of the Cunard Line. The

Above Cabin-class luggage is taken on board the *Queen Mary* at Southampton in 1948. In the background a Consular official examines passengers' visas.

Far left Fact meets fantasy: the *Queen Mary* carried the rich and famous in equal measure and stars could rub shoulders with statesmen in the cabin-class dining room. Here Cary Grant in a still from *Holiday*, 1938, poses in front of a Cunard poster advertising the *Queen Mary*'s regular sailings.

Left The cover of a pre-war Cunard brochure detailing the delights to be found in the *Queen Mary*'s tourist-class accommodation.

number and position of the funnels was traditionally credited with great importance by many
passengers. As John Maxtone-Graham has
explained, in describing the *Mauretania*: 'The
original design had been amended from three
to four at the last moment; there are still some
Cunard posters today with an artist's rendering
of the *Mauretania* sporting three stacks.
The *Mauretania* and the *Lusitania* were the first
British four-stackers, a popular silhouette that
Cunard would repeat with the *Aquitania*.'
Often the fourth funnel was non-functional,
existing primarily to reassure steerage passengers
who tended naively to choose ships by the
number of funnels they sported. Shipping lines
also deliberately perpetuated the myth that a
ship's power, speed and reliability were directly
proportional to the number of stacks. But as
Maxtone-Graham also notes, when the United
States Congress began to place restrictions on
immigration, 'companies wooed the mass
passenger with a new brand of funnelmanship
only slightly more sophisticated than before:
fewer and faster. Four funnels, comforting
for immigrants, were passé for tourists. So the
numbers game was reversed and it was the
Germans who led the way even before the
war. The Hamburg–Amerika Line laid
down a trio of enormous liners with three
funnels only.'

On the *Queen Mary*, the three towering funnels
viewed from the sports deck recalled the elegant
verticality of the *Mauretania*, which was a symbolic predecessor in many ways; even though the
number of stacks had been reduced, the capacity
for even greater speed was there. The profile of
the bridge continued that theme, as it was only
partially dictated by function; while simply a box,
sub-divided into the chart house, separate captain's and officer's chart rooms, a gyro-compass
room, a soundproof cabin for confidential con-
versations, and the wheel house, the distinctive
elongated curving eyebrow that fronts it all continues the streamlined theme of the graduated
funnels. Also following a precedent set by the
Lusitania and *Mauretania*, since the *Aquitania* had
a more rectilinear face to present to the wind,
this elegant eyebrow seems even more pronounced on the *Queen Mary*. This is due perhaps
to the gradual, stepped section of the ship that
culminates in the sports deck, and the use of a
higher first funnel to accentuate its profile, or the
relatively shorter visual, if not actual, distance

Opposite page A Royal Marine
band plays on the *Queen Mary*'s
sun deck as she prepares to
sail on her maiden voyage to
New York.

Top left Maiden-voyage
passengers indulge in an unde-
manding game of deck quoits.

Below Bell boys exercise
passengers' dogs on the sports
deck. On board the *Queen Mary*
even a dog's life was to be envied:
the ship was equipped with fully-
serviced kennels complete with
their own lamppost.

Above The wheel house which, when completed, represented the acme of technological and engineering excellence. The *Queen Mary* was equipped with the latest navigational equipment including gyro-compass and gyro-pilot. The gyro-compass gave a permanent indication of true geographical north acting independently of the movement of the ship. The gyro-pilot navigated an automatic course, detecting any variation and determining the amount of helm necessary to correct it. A wheel fitted to the unit (seen behind the officer on the right) enabled the system to be controlled manually if required.

between the wheelhouse and the bow, achieved by the position of the decks between them.

Bridge houses, projecting 12 feet out from each side of the ship, allowed an unobstructed view down each side of the vessel, while the exterior portion of the curved wing also provided a vantage point for a clear view forward. To assist visibility from the bridge, an ingenious method was devised for keeping this external look-out post free of wind. A so-called 'high pressure slot' running along the top edge of the eyebrow, like a handrail, was designed to allow the wind to enter a lower, wider flange. The pressure of the air was increased by being forced out through the narrower, upper edge, and the resulting draught shot

vertically upwards, forming an invisible screen of high pressure air powerful enough to force rain and snow over it, far above the heads of anyone standing outside on the bridge, even in a gale. Inside, 'marine wipers', or clear-view screens, were equal to the high pressure slot in originality, made from a detached circle of glass rotated by a small electric motor, and cleaned by a stationary bar as it moved.

The wheel house, which looks so antiquated today with its dual set of yacht-style steering wheels; brass megaphones for amplifying voice commands; manually-operated electric telegraphs for the engine room; docking, anchor and cable equipment; and navigational draughting boards

Left Looking along the forecastle deck towards the bridge. The anchor chains seen in the foreground were comprised of steel links 24 ½ inches long by 14 ¾ inches wide and made from material 4 ⅛ inches thick. Each link weighed approximately 225 pounds and formed a 150-ton chain supporting a 16 ton dreadnought anchor.

Overleaf A view forward of the verandah grill, which sat isolated at the after end of the sun deck like a perfect fragment of a modernist villa. In the evenings this was the *Queen Mary*'s most fashionable place to dine and dance, to see and be seen.

Above The verandah grill served as the *Queen Mary*'s à la carte restaurant, cocktail lounge and nightclub. It was an intimately-scaled space, only 29 feet long and 68 feet wide but was almost entirely lined with windows on three sides which gave it spectacular panoramic views over the open decks below. The room was arranged around a parquet dance floor, while the remaining areas were covered in a daring black Wilton carpet.

Below Etched-glass balustrades divided the room into upper and lower levels intended respectively for dining and dancing.

Opposite page The entire decoration of this space was orchestrated by Doris Zinkeisen who specified the gold and silver colour scheme and chose the carpet, furnishings and fabrics and designed its special features including the electrically-lit balustrade whose colours changed in time with the music being played.

in the chart rooms for determining course and direction, was advertised – with no irony surely intended – as 'the high-watermark of achievement', at the time the ship was introduced into service. The handcrafted aspect of the technology employed, even in this most critical area, is evident in the smallest detail, such as the depth-sounding equipment. Based on an echo-sounding technique, it includes a recording fathometer of the kind used on submarines at that time. The instrument, which gives a reading of the depth of the water below the vessel, records the profile of the ocean floor directly onto a roll of plain white paper, which is loaded into it the way film is loaded into a camera. It has a directness and simplicity that seem light years removed from the high-technology equipment used today.

Walking aft from the sports deck past various ventilator hoods and fans, past the second funnel

and the glass dome over the main lounge below, there are staircases down to the sun deck which stretches for hundreds of feet both to port and to starboard of the liner; the gravity davits for the lifeboats form an angular open canopy along most of the length on both sides of the ship.

Doris Zinkeisen adding the finishing touches to a painted mural in the verandah grill. This detail on one of the room's corner piers and its long counterpart on the forward end wall depicted a fanciful parade of characters drawn from the theme of 'Entertainment'.

Further aft, this deck terminated in one of the most social of the open spaces for cabin-class passengers, overlooked by the verandah grill which was to prove to be an immensely popular and smart nightspot. A light and airy room, 29 feet wide and 70 feet long, it had a semicircular fully-glazed wall that looked out to the expansive, after end of the sun deck eight feet below it, a terracing sequence of three smaller decks cascading down to the rounded stern, and the sea beyond. Always requiring advance reservations, the grill was intended as a dining room, supper club and cocktail bar, serving an à la carte menu that required a surcharge over restaurant meals which were otherwise included in the fare. A nearly-square dance floor in sycamore parquet, bordered with mahogany and pearwood inlay, and a final, wide band of ebonized hornbeam, was the focal point of the room which stepped up in tiers that echoed the layering of the decks immediately beyond. These terminated in a stage where the band was located, in front of a 1,000-foot-square mural by the young Scottish artist Doris Zinkeisen depicting pantomime, theatre and circus themes.

The change in level helped establish a sense of intimacy in the space; as did the detailing, which differed from the other public rooms in the ship in that, aside from the dance floor, it did not rely entirely upon the massive use of wood for continuity. In addition to the mural, Doris Zinkeisen specified the decorative scheme for the pilasters, rendered in silver etched in gold, and the ceiling in the same combination. The ceiling was further divided into three large bays, also in silver and gold, indirectly lit by fixtures which, along with those at the glass dividers used as railings between

the levels, changed colour in time with the music. This device of playing coloured light up through the etched glass of the balustrades, as well as using reflectors to throw it horizontally across the dance floor to illuminate the dancers' feet, combined with the solid-black Wilton carpet around the dance floor, the *risqué* quality of the painted mural, and the curved black and silver bar, made the room very *outré* and irresistible to late-night revellers.

Of all the *Queen Mary*'s public rooms, the verandah grill most accurately represented the more progressive aspects of social sensibility in the 1930s. Unlike the ship's larger and more conventional Art Deco spaces, which had an ambience that encouraged a more sober level of decorum, the verandah grill seemed, externally at least, to capture the amorphous 'New Spirit' that Le Corbusier had referred to in his work *Vers une Architecture* more than a decade before. While Le Corbusier was inspired by the efficiency of ocean liners and other anonymously-created engineering masterworks in the course of realizing his own, early style, which eventually led to such familiar modernist icons as the Villa Stein de Monzie at Garches and the Villa Savoye at Poissy, we know that the writings and buildings of Adolf Loos affected him even more. The verandah grill, with its spare symmetrical facade facing aft on to a clear expanse of teak decking, looks eminently Loosian, as if it had been magically transplanted in its entirety from a chic Viennese residential enclave planned by the master. To the dismay of many of his friends, however, Loos was an inveterate Anglophile, writing passionately about what he considered to be the infallible logic

Above Doris Zinkeisen's 1,000-foot-square mural in the verandah grill depicted pantomime, theatre and circus characters trooping across the canvas from left to right. This was the main decorative feature of the room, occupying the entire wall behind the raised dais where the dance band was positioned.

Above and below The cabin-class gymnasium featured a colourful frieze of caricatures by Thomas Webster of familiar sporting figures of the day, a detail which did not survive the *Queen Mary*'s first post-war refit.

behind each aspect of English life, in his short-lived journal *Das Andere* (The Other). While packing its pages with advertisements for everything from spiffy nautical gear, such as yachting caps, blazers and white wool trousers, to oatmeal, considered by him to be the perfect food, Loos also extolled the virtues of nannies and riding bicycles, which may help to explain why his journal didn't catch on. There is subtle irony, however, in the fact that, in spite of its limited exposure, *Das Andere* made a significant impact, precisely because of the audacity of its author's views, implanting a subliminal connection between Englishness, sailing and modernism, which Le Corbusier was later to expand upon. The story comes full circle on the sun deck of the *Queen Mary*, with its own Loosian villa in miniature, exposed as ship architecture only by the necessary expedient of a mast puncturing it through the middle. Undeterred by this annoying intruder, Doris Zinkeisen used the mast as the base for an internally-lit, banded chronometer that revolved around its head, rendered in 'virile peach and luna blue glass, sandblasted and etched'.

The mast in the verandah grill was seized upon by its designer as one of several not very subtle metaphors by which to convey the real subtext of the venue. Stewards' stories of the assignations that followed its 3am closing are now legion. In both location and decor, the verandah grill conveyed an impression of forbidden pleasure made accessible to a select few – the implicit, but suppressed, sensuality of the typical palette of materials found elsewhere in the ship being made much more explicit. This aspect of nocturnal romance, which must have been considerably abetted by casement windows with heated sills that provided an unobstructed view of moonlight on the water, has recently been captured in a vodka advertisement selected for viewing on British Airways' transatlantic flights. In it, a generic ocean liner rendered in *soignée* cartoon, with three red funnels banded in Cunard black, forms the setting for a series of chance encounters, with caricatures of men in tuxedos and women in Harlowesque spaghetti-strap platinum silk gowns predominating. On the *Queen Mary* after dark they would have undoubtedly been heading for, or from, the verandah grill.

Above The cabin-class gymnasium was equipped with a bizarre variety of exercise equipment, most of it of dubious aerobic value. Surrogate horses were provided for those missing their morning canter, and frustrated yachtsmen could satisfy themselves with a spring-loaded nautical wheel.

Below The tourist-class gymnasium was kitted out with an equally strange array of physically-challenging amusements, differing only in the level of finish of its panelling and decorations.

Moving forward on the sun deck, along the port side, the next series of rooms that the royal party viewed were the cabin-class gymnasium and the squash courts which were connected to it inboard, and then by lift or stairs to the cabin-class swimming pool on D deck below. On 'the ship of beautiful woods', even the gymnasium, which is usually thought of as having wood only on the floor today, was considered a likely candidate for panelling; indeed, the special issue of *The Shipbuilder* dedicated to the *Queen Mary*, described it as being remarkable chiefly for the variety of woods represented: 'The shaded effect is secured by the use of seven different timbers disposed in horizontal bands and ranging from dark American walnut, French walnut, teak, Australian oak and British oak to light ash for the top-most course. The various bandings are separated by narrow sections of silver-bronze metal which give a pleasant emphasis to the horizontal treatment.'

That emphasis was augmented by a colourful frieze of caricatures by Thomas Webster of sporting figures of the day, all of whom would presumably have been easily recognized by the type of passenger using the facility. The equipment provided was intended to be equally familiar. For those suffering severe withdrawal symptoms

Above and opposite The cabin-class swimming pool, located deep in the *Queen Mary* on D deck below the main foyer, was enclosed for use at all times of the year. The use of balconies and a vaulted ceiling helped to heighten the scale of the space and to alleviate the restrictions imposed by the distance between decks. Terracotta tile was used throughout, predominantly beige in colour, banded with green. The ceiling was covered in simulated mother-of-pearl whose sparkle enhanced the intended impression of lightness.

brought on by not being able to go out for a morning canter for a five-day stretch, two surrogate electric horses were provided, complete with rather unconvincing saddles and bridles looking pathetically thin on their barrel-like leather mounts. Even more absurd was a 'camel-riding' machine, which looked the same but was considerably higher, supposedly for those sheikhs on board suffering the same sort of anxiety. 'The nautical wheel', of equally dubious aerobic value, fulfilled a similar function for frustrated captains missing their yachts badly enough to substitute staring at horizontal bands of wood in lieu of a real horizon. Such diversion, masquerading as exercise, continued in the rowing machines, vibrating belts, vibrating chairs, pulleys and other paraphernalia that characterized the passive motorized approach to such installations at the time. The image of men in three-piece worsted

Above A series of etched-glass panels on the theme of 'Fish in an Aquarium', by Charles Cameron Baillie, adorned the forward end of the tourist-class swimming pool.

Right The tourist-class swimming pool was located at the after end of the ship, on F deck, close to the waterline. In contrast with the cabin-class pool it was a low, horizontally-emphasized space with a virtually flat ceiling plane.

Above In the tourist-class pool, ivory and blue predominated. The pool itself was lined with glazed faience tiling, off-white in colour, articulated with blue bands of the same material. Paving on the bathers' deck was carried out in a pale grey non-slip tile incorporating a buff ceramic mosaic. The walls were faced in cream and mother-of-pearl terrazzo in slabs framed in silveroid, while the octagonal columns were clad with slabs of blue smaltino, again held in silveroid frames.

Left The 'Pompeian Bath' at the Royal Automobile Club, London 1908–11 by Mewès and Davis. Designed 25 years before Arthur Davis' scheme for the *Queen Mary*'s interiors, it prefigured many notable ocean-liner swimming pools including that on the *Imperator* which was a fairly faithful reproduction.

suits and Homburgs exercising on electric horses is completely absurd today, when the level of individual exertion seems to be in inverse proportion to the increasingly sedentary nature of daily life. The swimming pool, more appropriately called a 'bath' in initial plans because it was relatively shallow, with a maximum depth of six feet at one end, continued this attitude of genteel ease. Enclosed within a 42 by 60 foot space, with viewing balconies running along both long sides, the 22 by 35 foot pool was more a social meeting place than a forum for serious exercise.

Largely due to the dominance of French architect Charles Mewès, who was encouraged by director Albert Ballin to design for the Hamburg–Amerika Line as part of Germany's bid to challenge Britain's monopoly on transatlantic travel at the turn of the century, swimming baths, along with the other more public rooms, had assumed great importance on such ships. Mewès' primary concern as an architect had been hotels, such as the Ritz in London which he completed in 1904, and gentlemen's clubs, such as the Royal Automobile Club in Pall Mall of 1908–11; and this connection became more generally established as his influence upon other maritime designers became stronger. Arthur Davis, whom Mewès relied upon as a collaborator in all his English work, was the chief interior designer of the *Queen Mary*, along with the American architect Benjamin Wistar Morris, and his experience with Mewès undoubtedly influenced this commission. Morris, on the other hand, was a fellow graduate of the Ecole des Beaux-Arts in Paris and had designed the grand Renaissance-revival Cunard Building on Lower Broadway in New York in 1921, amongst many other successful structures, and was employed to ensure that American taste would be well catered for in the *Queen Mary*'s interiors. The 'Pompeian Bath' which Mewès and Davis completed for the Royal Automobile Club, and which Mewès later reinterpreted on the *Imperator* and her two sister ships, is a *tour de force* which, while historically derivative, is spatially sophisticated and carefully proportioned and detailed. With its symmetrical

bi-level layout, based on a grand entry stair at one end, fountains, and coffered ceiling that cleverly gives the impression that the room has a greater vertical dimension than it actually possesses, it established a precedent that Davis followed in the *Queen Mary*'s cabin-class pool. Because the pool is enclosed for use at all times of the year, the problem of scale was critical, and the use of balconies and a vaulted ceiling helped to alleviate the restrictions imposed by the distance between decks. Davis continued his earlier tactics by using tile throughout, except on the ceiling which was executed in simulated mother-of-pearl, achieving the same effect of lightness that Mewès had managed to convey in his Pompeian Bath. The handmade terracotta tiles had individual profiles calibrated to account for the surrounding deck-loading at various points in the wall sections. They were mainly beige in colour while horizontal green bands and smaller faience tiles in pale blue formed a dado around the four large pillars that framed the space, and in the pool itself. A sandblasted glass panel by C Cameron Baillie, of cranes in flight against a red and green background, was originally incorporated into the front of the main stair, facing the pool.

The cabin-class pool balcony, corresponding to C deck, led on through revolving glass doors, to a suite of rooms called the turkish bath which was traditionally divided using classical designations into frigidarium, tepidarium, caldarium and laconicium, with steam room and massage

Opposite above Looking forward on the starboard side of the sun deck, adjacent to the engineering officers' accommodation. The openness and light of the sun deck offered a sharp contrast with the relative gloom of the promenade deck directly below.

Opposite below The *Queen Mary*'s promenade deck at the height of the ship's popularity in the late 1930s. At sea, the promenade deck became the maritime equivalent of the Via Veneto; *the* place to see and be seen and to rub shoulders with the rich and famous. It was here in March 1936 that Lord Burghley, the Olympic athlete, famously completed a full quarter-mile circuit of the ship in only 58 seconds, a remarkable achievement considering that the world record at the time was 49.6 seconds and the fact that he was weighed down by full evening dress. A brass plate was later affixed to the deck to commemorate the event.

Below An adjustable-type folding deck chair, as supplied by the Vono Company of Dudley Port, Staffs, for the *Queen Mary*'s promenade and sun decks.

ROWAN & BODEN LTD
SCOTTISH LEGAL BUILDINGS · GLASGOW

QUEEN MARY

DECK COVERING
DECK COMPOSITION
PLASTIC HARDWARE
CABIN FURNISHING
DECORATIVE PANELLING

LONDON · LIVERPOOL
BIRMINGHAM · NEWCASTLE

Above right An advertisement placed in the commemorative issue of *The Shipbuilder* by Rowan & Boden Ltd, suppliers of deck coverings, plastic fittings, cabin furnishings and decorative panelling aboard the *Queen Mary*.

Opposite Waring and Gillow of Oxford Street, London, was the chief contractor for the *Queen Mary*'s interiors, designing and supplying nearly all the furniture, and fitting out the majority of the staterooms. The company continued to specialize in liner interiors until the late 1960s.

room en suite. The colour of the terracotta tiles changed gradually after leaving the pool area, with progressively darker hues corresponding to the increasing temperature of each of the rooms, which varied from 80 to 200 degrees fahrenheit. The close connection between the pool and baths is historically based on the Hammam, which was, in turn, modelled after the Roman original which the Turks encountered after the capture of Constantinople, and this reiterates the leisurely, social premise of the ensemble. More adventurous passengers, however, particularly looked forward to rough weather, when the rolling of the ship would send waves crashing from one side of the pool to the other, upsetting the normally placid routine of paddling and splashing in relatively shallow water.

Mewès' legacy becomes increasingly evident on the promenade deck, one level below the sun deck, and the next stop on the royal tour of inspection of the ship. The promenade deck was a sheltered, glass-enclosed enclave of privilege, given over entirely to cabin-class passengers,

except for the tourist-class smoking room at its after end which was separated from the remainder of the deck by pairs of locked double doors. The promenade deck was to become an immensely popular public boulevard at sea, crowded with strollers who were fond of its sunny warmth and protection from wind and weather. Lined with deck chairs on its inboard side, it was the place to see and be seen, and to meet the most prestigious guests on the passenger list; it was the maritime equivalent of the Via Veneto at the height of its popularity in the late 1930s.

The cabin-class lounge was the most central of the promenade deck's great public rooms. Approached in design as the equivalent of the lobby of a grand hotel, with port and starboard galleries connecting it to the ballroom, smoking room and bar, the lounge was nearly square in configuration, and segmented spatially by changes in ceiling heights into one long rectangular central section flanked by lower side aisles. The high longitudinal central atrium was artificially illuminated to augment natural clerestory lighting, and anchored on its axis by a raised fully-equipped stage at one end and a fireplace at the other – a curious dichotomy of public entertainment and cosy domesticity, made all the more ambiguous by the original seating plan and furniture choices for the space, which were based on informal groupings around small pedestal tables and over-stuffed club chairs.

Autumn tints predominated in the colour scheme, produced by a combination of maple burr wall-panels with dados of makore. Above the stage proscenium was a gilt modelled group of musicians and singers, entitled 'Symphony', by Maurice Lambert, who also contributed some striking complementary panels over the entrance doors. When the parquet floor was not being used for dancing it was covered with a heavy-grade Wilton carpet and rugs in a leaf design executed in shades of dark green and grey.

The *Daily Telegraph* in a special *Queen Mary* supplement published on the day of the royal party's

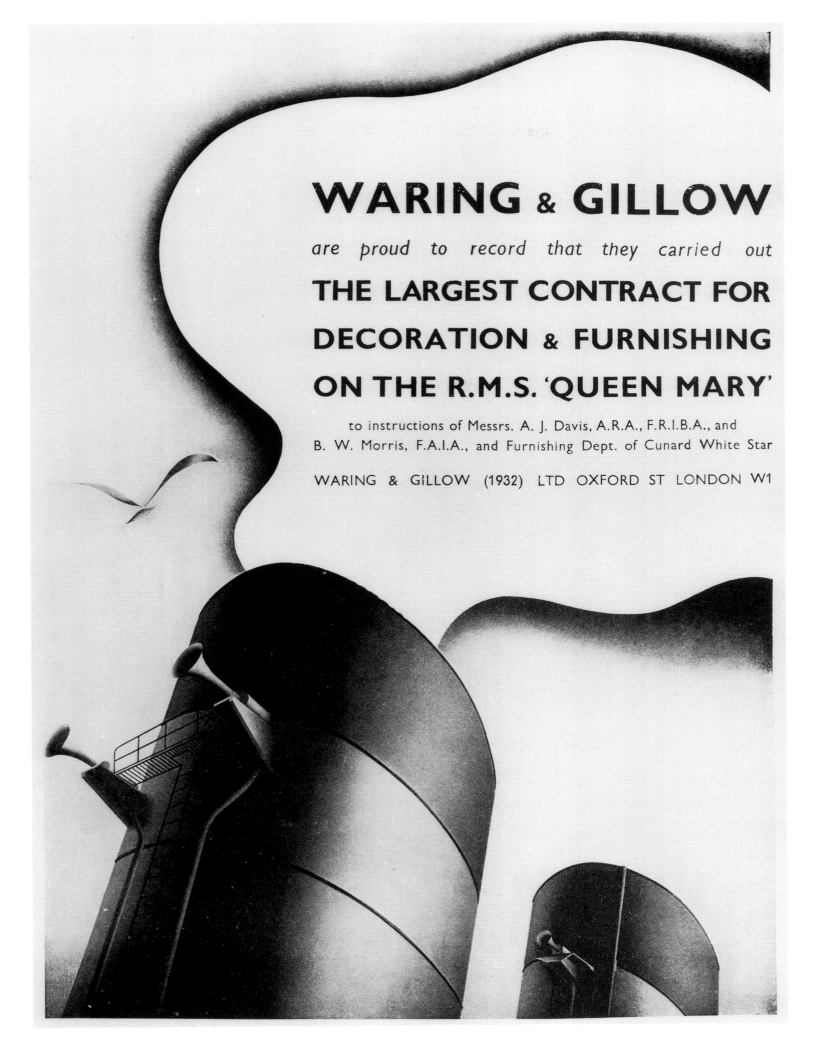

Opposite page A detail of 'Unicorns in Battle' by Alfred J Oakley and Gilbert Bayes, an enormous carved gesso panel which dominated the forward end of the cabin-class main lounge, framing an artificially-lit marble fireplace. Hinged doors in this panel opened to reveal film projection equipment, controlled from the cinema room behind.

Far left An artist's impression of the Queen Mary's main lounge c1935, advertising the fact that the room contained 'a deep-pile Wilton carpet of modern design'.

Left Stewards at work in the main lounge, cleaning the carpet and furniture, using the latest Hoover vacuum-cleaning equipment.

Below One of the dark alabaster torchières which originally provided soft uplighting in the main lounge.

tour noted that: 'Every visit to the *Queen Mary* confirms anew one's first impression of the extraordinary beauty of her decorative scheme. It may be affirmed without fear of challenge that never have the efforts of ship decorators, in collaboration with eminent exponents of contemporary art, achieved so great a measure of success. Thirty-three artists – painters, sculptors, wood and metal workers – whose names are well known on both sides of the Atlantic, have given of their best to the adornment of this noble ship. In the general scheme there is a complete absence of those ultra-modern effects whose appeal is confined to a small minority. Nowhere is there a hint of the fantastic.'

This sense of sobriety is perhaps due as much to those artists who declined Cunard's invitation as to those who accepted. Dame Laura Knight, Kenneth Shoesmith and Edward Wadsworth all contributed works; but Stanley Spencer, for example, turned down a commission, preferring to explore his own artistic interests rather than

work within the constraints of Morris and Davis' decorative scheme, while Duncan Grant was rejected outright by the Cunard directors.

A striking gesso panel above the curved onyx fireplace in the main lounge, by Alfred Oakley and Gilbert Bayes, depicts two 'Unicorns in Battle', with mountains in the distance. This ceiling-high panel, surrounded by walls covered in maple burr veneer, with a birch ceiling and wall recesses, uplit by dark alabaster *torchières*, provided one of the most memorable visual vignettes of the *Queen Mary*'s distinctive style; here as elsewhere natural materials, such as wood, were figured with others, such as the gold and silver gilt used in the panel. The furniture by Waring and Gillow was designed to reinforce the luxury and panache of this space. The tables were made of maple burr to co-ordinate with the walls, and most of the chairs had walnut backs, giving the entire lounge a warm, brown hue. The idea of rich panelled elegance was carried through the port-side long gallery which had

Above Two of a group of bronze-relief panels by Maurice Lambert which decorated the cabin-class main lounge. The largest of these was placed high above the stage proscenium at the after end of the room. Entitled 'Symphony', it featured a floating group of singers and musicians (*see opposite*). Smaller complementary reliefs were located above the double doors in each corner of the room.

22 floor-to-ceiling windows calibrating its entire 118 foot length looking out on to the promenade deck. These windows were draped to allow as much or little privacy as desired and to soften the character of what was, in reality, a transition or circulation space. Maple burr, with a makore surround, was used on the doors separating the lounge from the long gallery, whose furniture was, again, made in matching wood veneers. Sculptural *torchières*, approximately six feet high with yellow alabaster lenses similar to those lighting the glass panel above the lounge fireplace, punctuated the length of the room, adding an intermediate reference of human scale that subtly reduced its height.

The starboard gallery, like the long gallery on the opposite side of the ship, was entered from the lounge via a small lobby and served as an anteroom to the ballroom further aft. At 56 feet by 20 feet it was only half the length of the long gallery and was an intentionally cosier place for passengers of both sexes to retreat to between dances or after dinner. The room was decorated with a special laurel wood and the floor was covered with a Wilton rug in warm tones of brown. The windows were grouped in three bays, each containing three large windows draped with heavy curtains. On the long inboard wall were three large mural carvings by

John Skeaping executed in Honduras mahogany, treated with silver and gold. Decorative clocks were placed over the forward and aft doors, while above the fireplaces at either end of the room were painted flower studies by Cedric Morris.

While the starboard and long galleries were sober, the ballroom with which they both connected was exuberant, more in tune with the spirit of the verandah grill. It was a magnificent salon, 35 feet by 50 feet, its colour scheme of gold gleaming through a background of silver. The parquet floor was of Canadian wafla, with an inlaid-wood border, which was covered with geometric-patterned rugs when not being used for dancing. The windows overlooking the promenade deck were matched on the inboard, forward and aft walls by three large mirrored panels lit from behind and decorated with etched motifs. Between these mirrors and the windows, occupying the corners of the room, were painted murals by Anna Zinkeisen, sister of Doris Zinkeisen, featuring quasi-mythological treatments of 'The Four Seasons'. The double doors leading from the ballroom to the starboard gallery, as well as the two pairs of double entrance doors to the long gallery, were ornamented with large lacquer pilasters on a silver background with gold designs incised.

Above An artist's impression of the *Queen Mary*'s main lounge which featured in newspaper advertisements for holidays to the United States and Canada on board the ship in the late 1930s above the slogan: 'America and back in a fortnight – 6,000 miles in Britain's masterpiece'.

Left A view of the main lounge looking aft. A large and fully-equipped stage with a proscenium 26 feet wide by 22 feet high was one of the outstanding features of the lounge. It incorporated theatre lighting, wings and drop curtains and a cinema screen with the latest sound equipment. Before the installation of a purpose-designed cinema in the 1940s the lounge formed the main focus of the evening's entertainment on board the ship. The lounge could also double as a ballroom, the carpet being rolled back to reveal a parquet floor executed in oak panels with bands of mahogany and laurel. Magnificent windows, 13 feet high, lined the side aisles of this room giving views on to the promenade deck and the ocean beyond.

Right A detail from a 1936 advertisement placed by Wylie and Lockhead of Glasgow, announcing the fact that a splendid range of fabrics used in furnishing the *Queen Mary* could be obtained from the fabric department of their Buchanan Street store at prices from 4/6 per yard.

Far right A view of the cabin-class starboard gallery looking towards the double doors that gave access to the ballroom. Located aft of the main lounge on the promenade deck, this room served both as an ante-room to the ballroom and as a cosy space for passengers to retreat to between dances or after dinner.

"*Queen Mary*"
FURNISHING
Fabrics

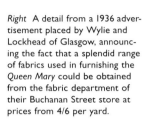

Above One of two painted flower studies by Cedric Morris which were originally placed above the fireplaces at either end of the starboard gallery.

Right The starboard gallery was panelled in laurel wood and fitted with a Wilton carpet in warm tones of brown, set in a parquet border executed in oak, mahogany and Indian laurel. This room fell victim to the *Queen Mary*'s first post-war refit; the space was reclaimed to make way for a purpose-designed cinema and projection suite.

'Deer Group' by John Skeaping. One of three mural carvings which originally decorated the starboard gallery's inboard wall. Executed in low relief in Honduras mahogany, these panels were relieved in silver and gold.

Opposite page A corner at the forward end of the long gallery, showing Bertram Nicholls' painting, 'A Sussex Landscape'. The seating arrangements here, as elsewhere on the ship, were intentionally informal, designed to suit small social groups.

Top left 'Evening on the Avon', by Algernon Newton, which dominated the after end of the long gallery.

Top right 'A Sussex Landscape' by Bertram Nicholls.

Left The long gallery formed the principal connecting space between the *Queen Mary*'s cabin-class main lounge, the ballroom and the smoking room further aft. Situated on the port side of the ship, it opened directly into the ballroom through two pairs of double doors. Lighting was provided by concealed cornice fittings supplemented by four large and four small illuminated pylons. Illuminated glass-panel windows on the inboard wall were intended to complement the great expanse of windows overlooking the promenade deck which occupied the full length of the 118-foot-long room.

Moving aft, the cabin-class smoking room, at the far end of the long gallery, resumed the wood-panelled, club-like theme, a reminder of the opulent woodwork that Mewès had often employed, in memorable rooms such as the social hall of the German liner *Vaterland*. Amusingly referred to as 'The Haven of the Male', in one Cunard brochure, the smoking room was described when first completed as, 'a lofty room, running through two decks, such a comfy, cosy place – so "oakish" and so English, just the sort of room that is popular with British and Americans alike: it seems to breathe the solid comfort of a typical English club or country-house smoking room. It is a room with alcoves, and comfortable leather-covered armchairs. In winter a real coal fire will blaze in the old-fashioned dug grate, which is the only coal fireplace in the ship.'

This 'oakish' feeling, which was actually achieved with native English pollard, chestnut, plain brown and combed oak – the favourite wood of Queen Victoria – helped to sell tickets as well as cigarettes. The entire ambience was carefully calculated to excite in the middle and upper-class American imagination an image of how an

Above and opposite Two panels from Anna Zinkeisen's quasi-mythological sequence 'The Four Seasons' which originally occupied the four corners of the cabin-class ballroom. The colours used complemented the overall scheme in the room; of gold gleaming through a background of silver. These panels were removed in the late 1940s when the ballroom was removed and the long gallery remodelled.

Right After the sober elegance of the starboard and long galleries, the ballroom provided an exuberant setting for a perfect evening of dancing. The parquet floor was elaborately laid out in cross-grain oak, with a wide border in sycamore, laurel and peartree. A raised platform, 35 feet long and 16 feet wide, was arranged at the starboard side of the room for refreshments, and balanced on the other side of the room by a corresponding dais for the use of the orchestra. The balustrade incorporated metalwork in silver and bronze and was topped with a handrail of pink hide. The central light fitting was a mass of prismatic lustres, with a base of sandblasted peach glass and a frilled top of tetra glass.

Opposite Large windows overlooking the promenade deck were matched on the ballroom's remaining three sides by large back-lit glass panels by Jan Juta. Their virile designs were executed in a variety of techniques including brilliant-cutting, acid etching and sandblast shading as well as ceramic enamel work.

English club might look, for the nouveau riche would never have the slightest chance of belonging to one. This patina of what was meant to be perceived as 'class' by the wealthiest members of a supposedly classless society, is as thin as the costly veneers meant to convey it, but it was effective, as the *Queen Mary* was one of the most commercially successful enterprises in the history of the Cunard Line. In spite of this rather transparent motive, of the anachronistic, Edwardian premise of the space, it was one of the most handsome of them all. Its soaring central foyer was surmounted by a large dome, lit by a light well projecting up through the sun deck, and separated by wood-wrapped columns from the surrounding, more intimately scaled space. The comfortable leather armchairs originally promoted by the Cunard public relations department, which had an office for a full-time

representative on board, just below the bridge on the sun deck, were unlike anything ever seen in any 'typical' London club, and were rendered in red, mauve, blue, beige and brown leather, continuing the pretence of trendy dis-tinction which this room particularly embodied.

Two pierced and carved screens flanking the fire-place were the work of James Woodford, who also contributed an elaborate decorative surround to the clock and a series of cast bronze electric light sconces with motifs of playing-card figures against a background of tobacco leaves. At either end of the room were striking, quasi-surrealist nautical paintings by Edward Wadsworth.

The tourist-class smoking room, isolated at the after end of the ship at this level, told another story entirely. It had a uniformly low ceiling, and

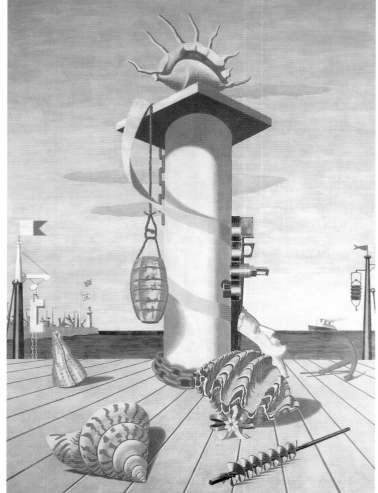

built-in settees upholstered in brightly-coloured, lozenge-patterned fabric, intended to provide 'the ideal setting for informal card parties', which looked out over vast expanses of synthetic korkoid instead of the plush pile found in its cabin-class counterpart. This undeniably practical, linoleum-like material, which was a rubberized composite of compressed cork, was used as flooring in the majority of the public rooms, staterooms, corri-dors and stairways throughout the ship, in a vari-ety of patterns and colours, providing a sterile contrast to 'the ship of beautiful woods' concept that Cunard successfully promoted.

In the tourist-class smoking room, the antiseptic impact of the korkoid was originally mitigated by banding it in alternating panels of black, cream and burnt sienna. Carpets were also carefully placed to foster the 'informal' gatherings envis-aged by the designers. This balanced approach between carpet and korkoid was also the general rule in most of the other public rooms in which

the material was used. The tourist-class smoking room is also notable as the original location of one of the most moving commissions to be carried out by any artist for the *Queen Mary*: the painting of the *Mauretania*, shown on her last voyage to be broken up at Rosyth on 4 July 1935, by Charles Pears. In contrast to Bertram Nicholls' bucolic Sussex scene of fields full of cows, and churches in the distance, and Algernon Newton's 'Evening on the Avon', used to prompt the nostalgia or encourage the Anglophilia of cabin-class passengers on their way through the long gallery to their clubby, smoke-filled enclave, this choice of a painting of one of the most pop-ular liners that Cunard had ever operated, was intended to convey a more robust image, depict-ing the ignominious end of a once-great liner.

The much-loved *Mauretania*, which may be seen as the stylistic precursor of the *Queen Mary* in many ways, and was known by the nickname of 'The Mary' to her staff and crew, was a hands-

BUOYANT GOES TO SEA..

For the giant Cunarder "Queen Mary" Britain's bid to beat all rivals in ocean speed and splendour, twelve hundred and sixty easy chairs and other upholstered pieces were made by Buoyant, who are proud to have shared in adorning so glorious a ship, proud to have shared in defining the limit in luxury.

BUOYANT
EASY CHAIRS and SETTEES

THE BUOYANT UPHOLSTERY COMPANY LTD., SANDIACRE, NOTTS

on, no-nonsense kind of ship which, for all its hard-working, functional pragmatism, was perceived as having great elegance. Pears' rendering captures this quality perfectly. The waterline view that the artist has chosen, as well as the accentuated verticality of the columns of black smoke pouring out of four slender stacks, clearly conveys the impression of power and style that faithful admirers remembered. Old age and escalating operating costs, which were eventually to contribute to the demise of all transatlantic passenger liners, including the *Queen Mary*, ultimately led to the decision to send the *Mauretania* to the breaker's yard; and Pears' painting, showing her at day's end, as the low angle of the sun makes the water sparkle, may perhaps be seen as prophetic. As John Maxtone-Graham has said: 'A landmark's destruction is predictably a matter of public emotional regret. In the case of the *Mauretania*, the urge for universal commiseration was particularly strong. Whether it represented the passing of an institution, a subtle reminder of the fragility of human endeavour or literally the death of a living thing is difficult to say.' In any event, this ascription of personality passed almost automatically to the *Queen Mary*.

The commercial complement of the plush, clubby interiors of the long gallery and cabin-class smoking room, was the more easily accessible group of shops bracketed by the first and second funnel hatches. The shopping centre on the promenade deck offered a wide selection of pricey gifts to cabin-class passengers, as well as cigars, cigarettes and flowers. There were branches of WH Smith and Austin Reed, where gentlemen passengers could invest in a white waistcoat or even a *Queen Mary* tie. Axially balanced between, at one end, a ceremonial stair leading down to the cabin-class entrance and suites on A deck, and the cabin-class accommodation on B deck below, and at the other end by a streamlined glass-enclosed, U-shaped shop projecting into the arcade, this was the place to acquire legally a souvenir of the voyage or to pick up presents for loved ones waiting at its destination. Wide expanses of highly waxed and polished, wood-toned korkoid,

were punctuated by perfectly round mast-like columns, fitted with chrome collars at the top, middle and bottom of the wooden shafts.

A large decorative fountain was originally placed here, complemented by huge *jardinières* containing fresh flowers. Maurice Lambert was responsible for the 50-foot-long ivory-toned plaster frieze. The walls were lined with fine figured chestnut coursed with plain chestnut bands above a dado in elm burr. Looking towards the main cabin-class staircase passengers were confronted with a large marble plaque of Queen Mary herself, carved by Lady Hilton Young.

The luxurious array of expensive gifts, incandescently lit in rounded custom-made wood and glass cases, gave this space an unmistakably nautical feeling, as if the Burlington Arcade had been adapted as the interior of a large yacht. As in the cabin-class lounge, where a stage competes with a fireplace for attention, this partially enclosed shopping promenade, usually referred to as 'Regent Street' by passengers and staff alike, was flanked by a library, on its port side, and a small chapel, called the 'drawing room', to starboard, which seems rather incongruous in this location. While the library continues the carpeted, panelled and curtained theme established in the long gallery, with books carefully ensconced in glass-fronted cabinets, the oval drawing room continued the domestic aspirations of the lounge, with a fireplace on its after end wall in onyx d'or surmounted by a decorative painting of a flower market by Kenneth Shoesmith. The hearth was built of Napoleon marble.

At the forward end of the room was an altar with a small sacristy and robing room, provided for Divine worship, although a non-denominational service was more usually conducted in the main lounge by the captain on Sunday mornings at sea. Screened off when the altar was not in use, the altarpiece painting, entitled 'Madonna of the Atlantic', was by Kenneth Shoesmith, who also executed the harbour scene over the altar's enclosing doors.

Opposite An advertisement placed in the commemorative issue of *The Shipbuilder* by the Buoyant Upholstery Company Ltd, suppliers of 'buoyant' armchairs and other furnishings for the *Queen Mary*.

Overleaf left Situated aft of the cabin-class smoking room, the tourist-class smoking room was the only major public room of this designation on the promenade deck. Noticeably less well-appointed than its cabin-class counterpart and with none of its spatial panache, it was nonetheless an elegant room, panelled in 'linenfold' brown curly oak with inserts of Indian gold padouk; the ornately-profiled columns and pilasters were lined with walnut.

Overleaf right Located above the electric fireplace in the tourist-class smoking room was Charles Pears' painting of the *Mauretania*, shown on her last journey to be broken up at Rosyth on 4 July 1935. This painting conveys a robust image, depicting the ignominious end of a once-great liner and seems at odds with the bucolic or fantastic works of art commissioned elsewhere on the *Queen Mary*.

Top right Looking axially along the main hall shopping centre from the main cabin-class staircase. Located between the forward and midships funnel hatches on the promenade deck, this was the place where passengers could browse in Austin Reed or WH Smith or simply purchase tobacco and souvenirs. There were originally 24 silver-bronze-framed showcases, the largest of which were 25 feet long. At the head of the staircase was Lady Hilton Young's portrait medallion of Her Majesty Queen Mary.

Right An illustration from the *Queen Mary* 'Book of Comparisons' extolling the merits of life aboard the new superliner. The shopping centre on board the ship was known popularly as 'Regent Street'.

Opposite page The lighting in the shopping area formed an integral part of the decorative scheme by Waring and Gillow. Concealed lighting in the soffit complemented a series of circular ceiling fittings and the special illumination of the shop-front vitrines.

Beyond the first funnel, and the children's play-room which ran the entire length of the star-board side of the funnel hatch, and was demurely divided between girls' and boys' sides connected by a chute, and decorated with a mural of teddy bears, trains and the man in the moon, was the observation lounge and cocktail bar, one of the most architecturally cohesive spaces on the entire ship. This impression of stylistic and volumetric unity may be due to the position of the room, as well as its comprehensible scale, made necessary by the restrictions that the funnel hatch on one side, and rounded forward end of the promenade deck on the other, imposed upon its designers, Waring and Gillow. The forward edge of the semicircular room, which is 34 feet wide at its axis and 70 feet long at its straight, inboard edge, was entirely rimmed with tall wood-framed win-dows, allowing an unobstructed view out onto the main deck below, and the bow beyond. As the forward equivalent of the verandah grill, the observation bar also incorporated the idea of cascading floor planes, which step up in stages towards the windows, linked by wide stairways of three easy steps each. While restricted to cabin-class passengers, this room had a more egalitarian air than the verandah grill, due largely to its longer hours of operation and its accessibility via a relatively short pair of corridors leading directly from either side of the shopping arcade. A mural by A R Thomson over the bar, 'The Royal Jubilee Week, 1935', offered a colourful cavalcade of London characters, reinforcing this popular theme. In marked contrast to the thinly-veiled sexuality of Doris Zinkeisen's paintings which dominated the verandah grill, Thomson illustrated

Opposite An etched and brilliant-cut glass impression of the *Queen Mary* in one of the windows of the travel bureau located next to the cabin-class entrance on the main deck.

Above and below Wrapped around the cornice of the central shop in the main hall was 'Sport and Speed' – a 50-foot frieze in ivory plaster relief by Maurice Lambert. Comprised of panels two feet high in varying lengths it depicted scenes of running athletes, bounding gazelles and speeding aircraft guided by ghostly impressions of the artist's own hands.

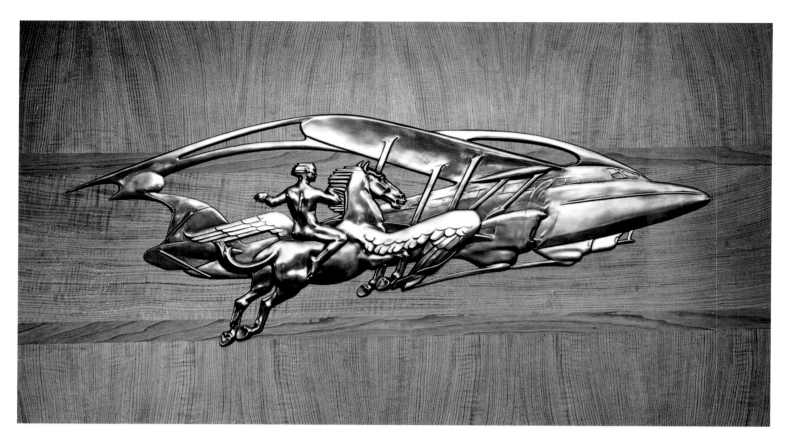

Above 'Speed and Progress' by Maurice Lambert; one of a pair of anodized aluminium reliefs by the artist located to port and starboard on the walls of the travel bureau. The theme of speed is an echo from that of the frieze in the main hall on the promenade deck above: here an Imperial Airways aircraft out-strips a rearing Pegasus.

Right The cabin-class entrance and travel bureau on the main deck. The doors on the right lead to the main staircase linking all levels of cabin-class accommo-dation. The door to the travel bureau can be seen on the left.

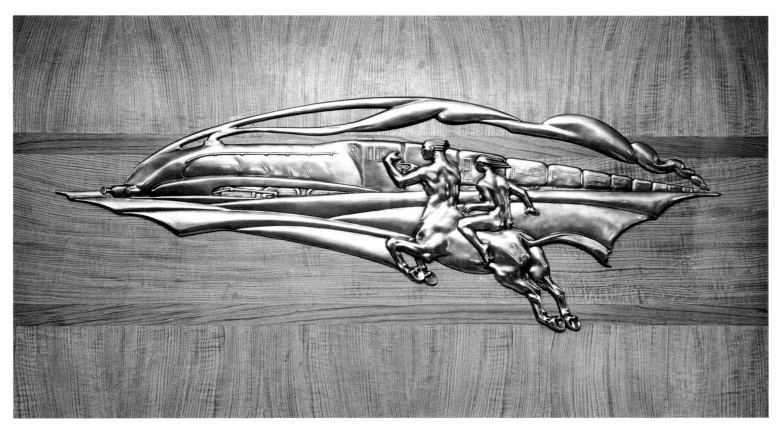

Above 'Speed and Progress' by Maurice Lambert; the companion piece to that shown opposite. In this panel, located on the port side of the travel bureau, the express train 'Silver Jubilee' is shown racing ahead of a galloping centaur.

Left The travel bureau as remodelled in the *Queen Mary*'s first post-war refit. The Maurice Lambert panels have been removed and the bureau has a more business-like, open-fronted arrangement.

'Madonna of the Atlantic', by Kenneth Shoesmith, painted for the cabin-class drawing room on the promenade deck. At the forward end of this room was an altar, with adjoining sacristy and robing room, which allowed its occasional use as a chapel. The 'Madonna', executed on a gold-leaf background, formed the altar-piece on such occasions. At other times it was concealed behind a folding screen bearing a painted harbour scene also by Kenneth Shoesmith.

Top A view of the drawing room looking forward towards the closed screen doors of the altar. The walls and ceiling of this modest room were painted in a pale grey gloss enamel. The lighting was indirect, the fittings being concealed in the ceiling soffit. The pedestal tables were veneered in rosewood and amboyna, with formica tops trimmed with metal. The floor was covered with dark blue rugs trimmed with gold. The carpet shown in this photograph is not original.

Far left Kenneth Shoesmith at work on the 'Madonna of the Atlantic' in his studio. The marine imagery of this painting is consistently pursued: the Virgin's halo appears to be a mariner's compass and an array of navigational instruments and charts lay at her feet. The globe is turned to the North Atlantic.

Left 'Flower Market' by Kenneth Shoesmith which surrounds a fireplace and mantelpiece in onyx d'or at the after end of the drawing room.

Right A stewardess arranges toys in the tourist-class children's playroom on the main deck. There were three such playrooms on board the *Queen Mary*, one for each class. The mural was executed by the well-known children's artist and writer Herry Perry.

Below left A detail from a mural painting by George Ramon in the cabin-class children's playroom, featuring performing teddy bears.

Below right 'Sinbad the Sailor' by Charles Cameron Baillie, one of two panels on this theme painted for the third-class children's playroom.

Opposite page A view of the cabin-class children's playroom looking aft. Divided into separate areas for girls' and boys' play it featured a chute which lead down from the boys' side to the centre of the room. A small aquarium, seen next to the chute, contained tropical fish. A miniature movie-theatre complete with press-button controls occupied the after end of the room.

a street scene showing the celebration of King George V's 25th year as king. In a panorama that included people from all walks of life, rotund society matrons join hands with sailors and workmen to cavort in front of a royal pavilion festooned with banners bearing the insignia of St George. The ebony arc of the bar, which is reiterated by a dropped cove of indirect, incandescent light above it, was the focal point of the space, providing a vibrant interior counterpoint to the distant views out to sea. Dark brown, maple burr walls fanning out from the bar, and running across the top of the line of french doors opposite, helped contribute to the embracing feeling of unity that the space conveyed, leaving a lasting impression of gaiety and warmth. Fresh flowers were replaced regularly by the gardener in highly ornate Art Deco *jardinières* flanking each of the stairways, providing an additional touch of elegance to a room that struck a fine balance between heaviness and lightness, inside and outside.

From the observation lounge, back across the shopping gallery, it was a short walk to the main stair down to the main deck, and the cabin-class suites which occupied its central segment, in the vicinity of the second funnel hatch.

These suites, consisting of a bedroom, sitting room and private bathroom were selectively

Opposite and above The semi-circular observation lounge and cocktail bar was one of the most architecturally cohesive of the *Queen Mary*'s great public rooms. It was divided into upper and lower levels to take account of the rising camber of the deck. The raised platform that ran around the forward edge of the room offered a splendid panoramic vantage point with views of the bow and the ocean beyond. Within the room, the main focus was provided by the Macassar ebony-fronted bar and the painting 'Royal Jubilee Week, 1935' by A R Thomson which was placed above it.

Opposite page The furniture in the observation lounge included round tables, and stools covered in red hide. The simple central supports were of nickel-chromium stainless-steel tube and were screwed to the deck. The remaining furnishings were designed and supplied by Waring and Gillow.

Top left The balustrade dividing the observation lounge's upper and lower levels was designed and executed by Austin Crompton Roberts. It has an eclectic thematic agenda, mixing wine casks, wildlife and maritime imagery in a free-spirited way.

Above A detail of a decorative ventilation grille from the observation lounge.

Left Four metal and enamelled pylons were incorporated in the balustrade and cast a soft uplight onto the ceiling.

Above A detail of a cabin-class bathroom. Services included the option of hot and cold salt or fresh water for baths, and the rooms were panelled in formica, then a new and fashionable material.

Canadian birch. The use of deal for this purpose is probably unique, as it is a soft wood and rarely, if ever, used for ship decoration. It has a particular charm as a background, which is possessed by no hardwood. It is traditional, in as much as the wood was used for decorative purposes throughout the latter half of the seventeenth and eighteenth centuries. Subsequently, rooms so decorated were stripped, and this gave rise to the recent vogue for natural-pine rooms and furniture.' In line with this convoluted rationale, through which the use of a cheaper material was justified as being at once 'traditional' and 'in vogue', the carpets are praised as 'being almost a natural undyed sheep's wool' in order to maintain the neutral, off-white background against which the special suites could be established. The rugs were 'handtufted' just as the curtains were 'handwoven'.

It was Cunard's proud boast that almost every passenger's tastes could be catered for. The Duke and Duchess of Windsor, for example, always booked the same suite of staterooms aboard the *Queen Mary* – number M58 on the main deck – and the chief steward would arrange for them to be re-equipped with curtains and covers in the Duchess' favourite electric blues and greens.

In contrast to the massive marble panelling, tubs and sinks, and tile floors that were common in Hamburg–Amerika liners before World War I, such as the *Imperator*, the bathrooms in these suites, as in all the guestrooms of the *Queen Mary*, were mainly fitted out with synthetic materials, such as faux-alabaster surrounds and formica wall-coverings, and enamelled metal baths, in order not only to reduce weight and cost, but also to improve speed. As an extra, and significant gesture towards fresh-water conservation and thus weight reduction, salt water was available in addition to fresh water for baths and showers, providing an alternative which many passengers seemed to prefer, since a hot, salt-water bath was a luxury usually unavailable on land. This varied in tourist class, where salt water only was available.

decorated to give each its own personality, and were named accordingly. The basic shell was panelled in light Honduras mahogany, with ivory-satin curtains and bedspreads and wall-to-wall carpeting overlaid with custom-woven rugs to match individual furnishings. The furnishings included four-feet six-inch-wide beds with large wooden headboards, wardrobes, dressers with mirrors, writing tables, bedside tables with lamps, easy chairs and dressing stools. As much as possible, the surfaces on all furniture were flush, to reduce wear and breakage, and to convey the desired effect of modernity felt to be of primary importance by the designers. In some of the suites, this attitude, undoubtedly abetted by the desire to economize, led to a different approach. As described in the special volume of *The Shipbuilder* dedicated to the *Queen Mary*'s maiden voyage: 'in some cases the woods selected were of the lightest possible colour, viz, deal (commonly called pine), bird's-eye maple and

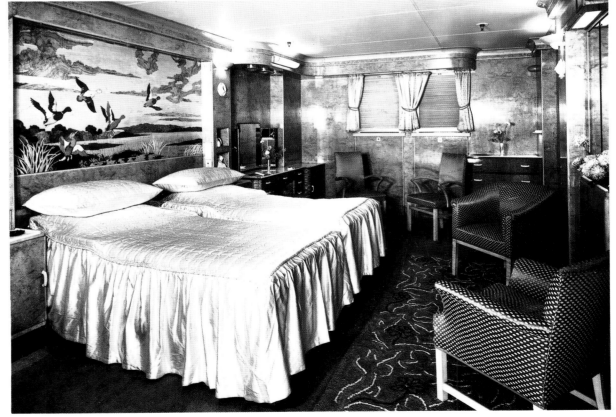

Left Among the cabin-class staterooms on A deck were a number of special suites, each consisting of a bedroom, sitting room and private bathroom. They were arranged so that, when the occasion arose, the sitting rooms could serve as bedrooms. The photograph above shows a sitting room with its original furnishings and rugs; the lower picture shows the same room refitted as a bedroom in the 1940s. Specially-commissioned artworks, like the complex marquetry panel in this room, were a significant feature of all such staterooms.

Above A decorative statuette from a cabin-class stateroom.

Above right and right Interiors of two of the special cabin-class stateroom suites on A deck. All these rooms were panelled, mostly in light woods such as deal, bird's-eye maple and Canadian birch. The furniture, with the exception of chairs and stools, was entirely fitted and featured flush and rounded details in the same material as the walls. The ceilings were devoid of ornament, and finished in a pale ivory enamel. Light fittings and other metalwork were of silver-bronze and the glass in the fittings was white sand-blasted, to give a gentle even spread of light.

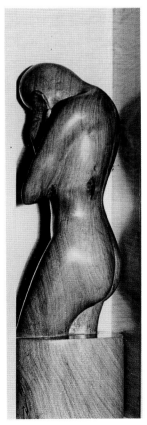

Left A cabin-class stateroom in one of the midship suites on the main deck. Various decorative treatments were employed in these suites, ranging from mahogany or light wood panelling to combinations of woodwork, fabrics and coloured paints.

Below left A sitting room in one of the special cabin-class suites. Each of the 54 special staterooms on the main and A decks were individually designed and employed such decorative novelties as peach glass and python-skin fabrics.

Below This decorative statuette, executed in walnut, was located within a maple-panelled niche in one of the special cabin-class suites.

Above right An illustration from the *Queen Mary* 'Book of Comparisons': 'Perhaps the single feature of the new *Queen Mary* which will most impress a passenger with her extreme modernity, is the fact that he can pick up the telephone on the bedside table of his stateroom and talk with friends in New York, London, Paris ... or any other part of the civilized world.'

Right The actress Marion Davies makes a telephone call from her stateroom.

The designers favoured L-shaped configurations for the special cabin-class suites in the middle of both the main and A-deck levels, because they allowed the most efficient disposition of the additional sitting rooms, and even servants' quarters and 'box rooms' for wardrobe trunks. Each suite had an outboard ocean view. As the plan of the ship narrowed further forward and aft, space became more limited and these cabins were offered as single-berth rooms only. All were provided with electric renditions of coal-burning fireplaces, as well as 'Thermo-Reg' ventilation, by which each room received cold or warm air through individual ducts.

Great emphasis was placed in Cunard's promotional brochures, on the innovatory telephone service, which was available in every cabin class room, with room-to-room, or ship-to-shore contact in Europe or America being possible. This capacity kept an entire platoon of operators working shifts at the ship's switchboard, busy 24 hours a day, serving the *Queen Mary*'s 600 telephone lines with little respite. The wireless receiving station that made all this possible utilized 32 wavelengths including seven for long-wave communication, with nine aerials set aside for this purpose. Radio broadcasts received on this system were re-distributed throughout the ship via 38 loud speakers, as well as individual speakers in each room, as was dance music, being played in any one of several locations including the ballroom and the verandah grill.

In contrast to the cabin-class staterooms, those in tourist class, which were arranged over five decks from A to E, and intended for two, three or four people, typically had narrower, three-foot-wide beds, as well as fold-out Pullman berths in some instances. About 80 per cent of the tourist-class rooms, which were also mostly outboard, had bathrooms but with much less wood in evidence. Green, blue and gold colour schemes replaced the sleek ivory interiors of the cabin-class staterooms. Third-class cabins, which were proportionally greater in number on the *Queen Mary* than on previous Cunard liners, as the company

made its bid for that segment of the market, were enthusiastically promoted as having 'not the slightest suggestion of overcrowding', and yet had to rely upon more traditional, bunk-style sleeping arrangements, and outside bathrooms to attain even a minimally acceptable standard. In a typical, eight foot by ten foot cabin, a pair of curtained three-foot-wide stacked bunks would occupy one wall leaving a narrow passage in the middle, and space for a pair of chairs opposite. A wash stand, small dresser and mirror completed the basic ensemble. The floors were of purple korkoid, a colour choice with myriad associations – those the designers had in mind can only be guessed at.

One of the last, and most spectacular, sights confronting the royal party on their tour of the brand new ship as they moved from the sports deck to the exit on C deck, six levels below, was the cabin-class restaurant, the stylistic result of a long tradition of luxurious dining rooms that had evolved in ocean liners since the turn of the century. At 118 by 160 feet, the slightly square space

Left Operators busy in the radio control room. The low-frequency transmitting and receiving equipment on board the *Queen Mary* was more powerful than on any previous ship. Regular radio programmes from American and European stations could be picked up and distributed through 38 loudspeakers divided into eight separately controlled groups allowing passengers to choose from a variety of the best features on the air.

Above A typical outboard tourist-class stateroom. Smaller and plainer than their cabin-class equivalents, they relied on painted finishes and fabrics for decorative effect.

Below An advertisement for 'Beautyrest' mattresses as supplied for the *Queen Mary*.

Left An inboard third-class cabin with Pullman folding upper berths. Built-in wardrobes and dressing tables with mirrors were supplied in each cabin along with wash basins, but there were no en-suite baths or lavatories.

Below left A typical outboard, twin-berth third-class cabin.

Below An advertisement for 'Somnus' mattresses as supplied for the *Queen Mary*.

Overleaf MacDonald Gill's monumental map of the North Atlantic which dominated the forward end of the cabin-class restaurant. Originally a crystal replica of the *Queen Mary* moved across the map, indicating her position at sea on her summer and winter courses.

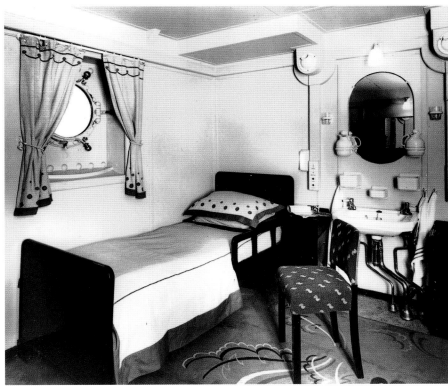

In extending our good wishes to all who may travel in

R.M.S. QUEEN MARY

we would express our pride in having contributed to the

luxurious comfort of this magnificent ship by the provision of

SOMNUS MATTRESSES

and equipment.

Ask your furnisher for Somnus·guaranteed Mattresses as supplied to R.M.S. Queen Mary, or write to The Bedding House of Rhodes, Carlton Cross Mills, Leeds, 2. And at Nottingham and Manchester. London Showrooms: 26, 27 Lawrence Lane, Cheapside, E.C.2.

Above Cabin-class passengers dining in the restaurant on the *Queen Mary*'s maiden voyage.

Opposite Looking forward along the high central nave of the restaurant towards MacDonald Gill's decorative map.

avoided the possibility of static proportions by rising to over 30 feet in successive stages, to a dome at the top. Sized to accommodate more than 800 passengers at one sitting, this was the largest public space ever built on a ship and the usual superlatives were employed to advertize the fact. Fanciful drawings of Samuel Cunard's original 1840 *Britannia*, along with Columbus' *Nina*, *Pinto* and *Santa Maria*, promoted the notion that they could fit inside the space with room to spare.

Included in the restaurant space were four private dining saloons, two at the forward end and two aft, decorated with paintings by Dame Laura Knight, Duncan Carse, H Davis Richter, and Agnes Pinder-Davis who also designed rugs and carpets and chose many of the fabrics for the *Queen Mary*'s public rooms.

In the main restaurant itself, the decorative scheme was in three shades of peroba wood whose mellow-gold colour was periodically articulated by silver-bronze bands. The soffits of the various lower levels, as they stepped up toward the centre, were sheathed in mazur birch veneer which, like the walls, took on a golden glow when lit by the incandescent fixtures on the ceiling above. The ubiquitous korkoid, in russet tones, completed the warm brown colour palette. A conspicuous feature of this space was a 15 by 24 foot map by MacDonald Gill, showing the *Queen Mary*'s summer and winter courses across the North Atlantic. England and America are caricatured on either side by buildings meant to express the historical difference between the two countries: England has St Paul's Cathedral and Big Ben while the United States has skyscrapers. An illuminated clock occupied the upper right-hand corner of the midnight blue and white chart, and a small crystal replica of the *Queen Mary* moved across it to represent its relative position at sea, reiterating the theme of speed, just as the MacDonald Gill's intentional foreshortening of the ocean distorted and

Opposite page A detail from the bronze double doors in the cabin-class restaurant by Walter and Donald Gilbert.

Far left Hand-engraved and silvered plate glass panels on the theme of 'Jason and the Golden Fleece' by Jacob Drew.

Left The painter and sculptor Bainbridge Copnall contributed a series of ten carved wood-relief panels for the cabin-class restaurant, based on the theme of 'Ships through the Ages'. Shown, centre, is one of the largest of this group, with representations of three great Atlantic liners, the *Great Eastern*, *Mauretania* and *Queen Mary*.

reduced distance. At the after end of the hall, cast-bronze doors by Walter and Donald Gilbert counterbalanced the impact of the chart. Surmounting these doors was a painting in tapestry technique by Philip Connard RA depicting English country life and scenes. In addition, two painted panels on the inboard face of the ventilator shafts servicing the room, illustrated English and American birds against a background of silver leaf, and silvered plate-glass panels relayed the myth of Jason and the Golden Fleece. A series of carved-wood plaques created around the theme

of 'Ships through the Ages' completed the handcrafted artworks commissioned for the space, although the furniture also played an important role in defining its character. The *Daily Telegraph*, in a special supplement, noted that: 'Great care has been taken in the design of the special sycamore chairs, which are upholstered with show backs in a delicate rose pink, an ideal colour for setting off ladies' dresses to the best advantage.'

A master of description, Evelyn Waugh, who travelled on the *Queen Mary* in the 1930s,

Above An artist's impression of the cabin-class restaurant, looking aft towards the entrance doors. The painted panel, 'Merrie England', surrounding them is by Philip Connard RA, and was executed in a faux-tapestry technique.

Right Lipton advertised its teas using the *Queen Mary*'s restaurant as a background. Many other grocery suppliers similarly took advantage of the cachet attached to the new ship.

satirized this room, and the ambience of the majority of its public spaces in general when, through the eyes of Charles Ryder in the novel *Brideshead Revisited* he observed:

'I turned into some of the halls of the ship, which were huge without any splendour, as though they had been designed for a railway coach and preposterously magnified. I passed through vast bronze gates on which paper-thin Assyrian animals cavorted; I trod carpets the colour of blotting paper; the painted panels of the walls were like blotting paper too – kindergarten work in flat drab colours – and between the walls were yards and yards of biscuit-coloured wood which no carpenter's tool had ever touched, wood that had been bent round corners, invisibly joined strip-to-strip, steamed and squeezed and polished; all over the blotting paper carpet were strewn tables designed perhaps by a sanitary engineer, square blocks of stuffing for sitting in and upholstered, it seemed, in blotting paper also; the light of the hall was suffused from scores of hol-

Above and left The great bronze entrance doors to the restaurant were the work of the sculptors Walter and Donald Gilbert, a father and son partnership, who also executed similar doors leading to the private dining saloons at the forward end of the room. Arabesques represent the ocean while the vignettes within are drawn from classical mythology and all allude to the sea in some way. The left-hand door depicts Castor and Pollux, twins of the Gemini constellation, Siren enchantresses, and the three Graces, handmaidens to Venus who was born of the sea. At the base is a Triton. The right-hand door illustrates Europa's abduction by Jupiter who has changed into a bull; below are Latona and her children Apollo and Diana atop a dolphin; lower down is the birth of Venus; and at the base a Nereid.

MOTIF IN ANODYSED ALUMINIUM BY MAURICE LAMBERT.
MAIN DECK—R.M.S. "QUEEN MARY".

BREAKFAST

California Figs in Syrup   Compôte of Rhubarb   Baked Apples
Compôte of Figs   Compôte of Prunes
Grape Fruit   Apples   Oranges   Bananas   Pears
Orange Juice   Prune Juice   Tomato Juice

Cream of Wheat   Quaker Oats   Oatmeal   Bran Flakes
Rolled Oats   All Bran   Bonny Boy Toasted Oats   Post Toasties
Force Whole-Wheat Flakes   Shredded Wheat   Grape Nuts

Onion Soup Gratinée   -   *(To order 10 minutes)*

Fried Fillets of Whiting   Grilled Codfish-Parsley Butter
Kippered Herrings   Finnon Haddie in Cream

Eggs:—Boiled, Fried, Turned, Poached and Scrambled
Shirred Eggs and Grated Tongue   Omelettes Various

Hashed Chicken and Mushrooms   Scotch Collops and Poached Egg
Sauté Calf's Liver Sauce Robert

FROM THE GRILL *(To order)*
Ham Steaks-Devilled Sauce   Lambs Kidneys on Toast
Palethorpe Sausage   Tomatoes
Pale and Smoked Wiltshire and Irish Bacon   Wiltshire and York Ham

Potatoes:—Lyonnaise   Mashed   French Fried   Saratoga

ASSORTED COLD MEATS

SALADS   Tomatoes   Watercress   Spring Onions   Radishes

CAKES   Buckwheat and Griddle Cakes   Waffles - Maple Syrup

BREADS VARIOUS   White and Hovis Rolls   Brioches   Crescents
Soda Scones   Triscuits   French Toast   Sultana Buns

Conserve   Honey   Honey in the Comb   Marmalade

Tea:—Indian, Ceylon and China   Coffee   Cocoa
Cadbury's Cup Chocolate   Horlicks Malted Milk - Plain or Chocolate

Cunard
White Star

PRINTED IN ENGLAND.   Q C E. 2

Opposite page above 'The Mills Circus' by Dame Laura Knight which originally hung in one of the private dining rooms adjacent to the main cabin-class restaurant. In the early 1960s it was moved to the new 'midships bar' on the promenade deck where it formed the centrepiece behind the bar.

Opposite page below 'Birds of the Old World', by A Duncan Carse. This painted panel, featuring a white peacock and a variety of native pheasants, was located in the centre of the port-side wall of the restaurant. It was balanced on the starboard side by another canvas by Duncan Carse, entitled 'Birds of the New World'.

Left A breakfast menu, dated Friday 7 May 1937, and printed on board the *Queen Mary*. The decorative panel at the top is a coloured photographic print of Maurice Lambert's anodized aluminium panel 'Speed and Progress', to be found in the cabin-class entrance hall on the main deck.

"STAYBRITE"

SUPER STAINLESS

STEEL

ABOARD THE "QUEEN MARY"

FIRTH-VICKERS STAINLESS STEELS, LIMITED, SHEFFIELD

Here, there and everywhere throughout this great ship you will find that "STAYBRITE" Steel has been utilised for one or the other of its characteristics—corrosion resistance, mechanical strength or permanent aesthetic beauty of surface. For instance, throughout the kitchen and the various food preparing rooms "STAYBRITE" Steel plays its important part in ensuring cleanliness, hygiene and labour saving—a wonder metal throughout a wonder ship.

CABIN CLASS, COLD PANTRY AND COFFEE ROOM

Top left Crystal tableware manufactured for the *Queen Mary* by Stuart & Sons of Stourbridge; in all there were 22,000 pieces of table glass on board.

Middle left A china table service supplied by Jackson & Gosling Ltd of Stoke on Trent; the *Queen Mary* carried approximately 30,000 pieces of this service alone.

lows, giving an even glow, casting no shadows – the whole place hummed from its hundred ventilators and vibrated with the turn of the great engines below.'

Invisible to the diners in the restaurant were the kitchens which Queen Mary toured with the other ladies of the royal party. These were the antithesis of the pomp and circumstance that

Waugh depicted, part of the mechanical netherworld that existed discreetly just through double metal doors. Clad in yards of nickel-chromium and stainless steel, the kitchen was divided into the cabin-class section in the forward part, with the tourist-class section behind it, although the division imposed by economic level was imperceptible in this functionally-neutral zone. For the sake of efficiency, both kitchens were planned

Opposite page top right An advertisement for 'Staybrite' stainless-steel kitchen fittings, showing the *Queen Mary*'s cabin-class cold pantry and coffee room.

Opposite page bottom left A page from the 'Book of Comparisons' illustrating the extraordinary statistics of the ship's household equipment.

Opposite page bottom right Two-tier electric ovens in the *Queen Mary*'s bakery.

Above left Chefs at work in the *Queen Mary*'s kitchens; note the spartan quality of these spaces and their extreme contrast with the luxury of the restaurant and dining rooms beyond the swing doors.

Left A chef selects sides of meat from the larder.

to share such services as the vegetable preparation area, bakery and pastry preparation, and the dishwasher which drew no class distinction when dirty plates were piled into it from both directions.

The hyperbole commonly employed to impress the public with the *Queen Mary*'s enormous size, inevitably increased in descriptions of the refrigerated storage rooms, where food for each voyage was kept, since this was one of the most basic and easily identifiable things people could relate to. In its 60,000 cubic feet of space, Cunard was quick to disclose, were to be found:

'the 70 tons of meat required for every trip, with 14 butchers in adjacent butcher shops waiting to cut it into the necessary joints, as well as 20 tons of fish in its own room, and elsewhere 4,000 gallons of milk. In the poultry department, 4,000 chickens and ducklings are stored, and there are 3 tons of butter and 2,000 lbs of cheese. There is a special fruit-ripening room and storage elsewhere for 600 crates of apples and oranges. There are 70,000 eggs, 4,000 lbs of tea and coffee, and 10,000 lbs of sugar. In the ship's wine cellars are 10,000 bottles of wine, 40,000 bottles of beer and 60,000 bottles of mineral water, as well as 6,000 gallons of draught ale, 5,000 bottles of spirits, 5,000 cigars of all brands and 20,000 packets of cigarettes.'

After tea, having literally seen the ship from stem to stern, the royal party departed offering congratulations to its owners and captain, and wishing them a smooth maiden voyage, and the ship a long, productive career. Two days later, the *Queen Mary* left the Ocean Dock in Southampton to a jubilant send-off on its maiden voyage with 1,742 passengers and 1,186 crew on board. Prior to departure, more than 15,000 people had come to visit the new ship including nearly 300 visitors from across the Channel who were curious to see this rival to the *Normandie*, the French entrant in the North Atlantic sweepstake in which the prestige of each nation seemed to be inextricably entwined. The long-awaited event, anticipated by Britain since work on the liner had stopped

over five years before, was finally taking place. The high level of public anticipation that accompanied it was reflected in a week of gala *Queen Mary* dinners held at the Trocadero.

The maiden voyage, which began appropriately at tea-time on Wednesday 27 May, was heavily advertised by Cunard who felt that it was necessary to outdo the ballyhoo surrounding the departure of its rival, the *Normandie*, one year earlier. For several months preceding the event, on both sides of the Atlantic, the customary frugality, reticence and modesty of the company were momentarily forgotten as an unprecedent-

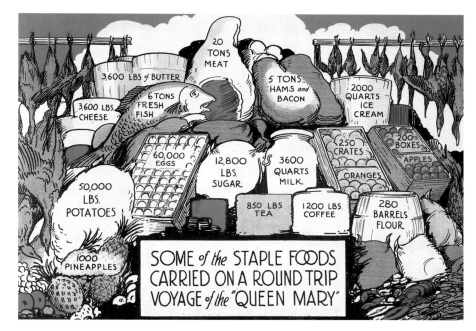

ed amount of promotional paraphernalia was released, including mountains of eight inch by ten inch glossies, posters and models of the ship, and incessant coverage of its impending departure and arrival, by both the European and American press. An American soap company sponsored a competition offering a prize of a free return passage in cabin class for anyone who could guess the length of the ship, which wasn't exactly secret at the time, and florists did a brisk business in *Queen Mary* bouquets.

In London *The Times* noted stiffly that among the passengers who had signed up early for the

Opposite page Sacks of flour being loaded aboard the *Queen Mary* by crane at the Southampton quayside. Turn-around times between voyages were incredibly short, essentially so if the weekly schedule was to be maintained. The *Queen Mary* would typically spend only one day in port in New York, and two days in Southampton, during which time one set of passengers would be disembarked and a new set welcomed, and all the ship's stores, provisions, fresh water and fuel for four days at sea would be loaded.

Above A page from the 'Book of Comparisons' showing some of the staple foods loaded on board the *Queen Mary* preparatory to a four-day voyage, and the extraordinary quantities required to feed 2,000 passengers and nearly 1,000 crew.

Overleaf The *Queen Mary* makes her maiden arrival in New York harbour on 1 June 1936.

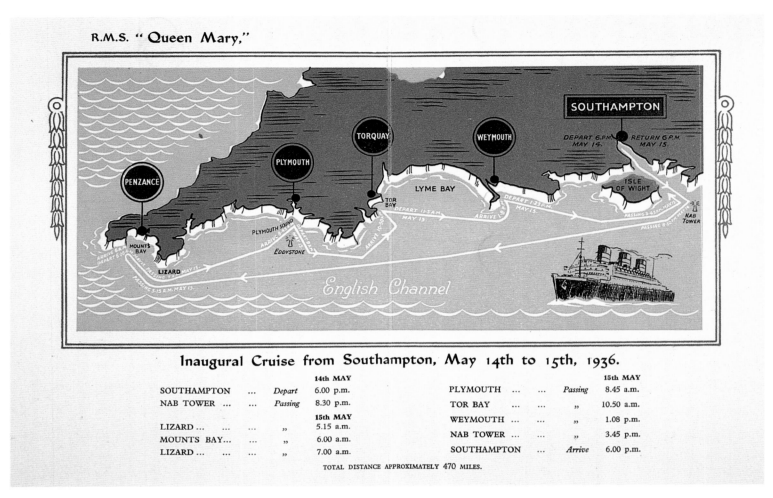

R.M.S. "Queen Mary,"

Inaugural Cruise from Southampton, May 14th to 15th, 1936.

			14th MAY					15th MAY
SOUTHAMPTON	...	Depart	6.00 p.m.	PLYMOUTH	...	...	Passing	8.45 a.m.
NAB TOWER ...	...	Passing	8.30 p.m.	TOR BAY	...	...	,,	10.50 a.m.
			15th MAY	WEYMOUTH ...	...	...	,,	1.08 p.m.
LIZARD ...	...	...	,, 5.15 a.m.	NAB TOWER ...	...	...	,,	3.45 p.m.
MOUNTS BAY...	...	,,	6.00 a.m.	SOUTHAMPTON	...	Arrive		6.00 p.m.
LIZARD ...	...	...	,, 7.00 a.m.					

TOTAL DISTANCE APPROXIMATELY 470 MILES.

Above A souvenir map of the *Queen Mary*'s inaugural cruise from 14 to 15 May 1936. This was a 'dress-rehearsal' for her maiden Atlantic crossing and an opportunity for the crew to get to know the ship. It was on this cruise that Lord Burghley made his record run around the promenade deck.

maiden passage to New York were: 'Viscount and Viscountess Knollys, the Marquess and Marchioness of Milford Haven, Lord Grimthorpe, Lord Inverclyde, Lord Marks, Sir Joseph Bell, Sir John Courtis, Lady Dent, Admiral Sir Richard and Lady Webb and Colonel G S Brocklebank.'

Fares in cabin class were advertised at £53.15s single and £102 return, with tourist class almost half that price at £28.10s single and £52.10s return. Third-class passengers could travel for a modest £18.10s single and £33.10s return. These fares applied throughout the year with the exception of the peak season between 3 August and 21 September when they increased slightly to £56.10s and £30 for a single passage in cabin and tourist class respectively.

The *Queen Mary* made the run from Cherbourg to the Ambrose Light Vessel in four days five hours and 24 minutes at an average speed of 29.13 knots, taking two hours and 32 minutes longer than the *Normandie* had managed the previous year. Having left Southampton to the strains of 'Rule Britannia' played by the Royal Marine Band, the liner was greeted by thousands of New Yorkers upon arrival on 1 June, many of whom had crowded on to pleasure boats to accompany her into the harbour. More than 100 journalists, as well as representatives of the BBC and other networks, were on board, and live broadcasts from every conceivable location were heard on both sides of the Atlantic.

In spite of the initial disappointment over the less than record time, there were, as Leslie Reade has observed, 'more accompanying boats, more noise, more general excitement, and although the official, top-ranking visitors in the *Normandie* had evoked more important hospitality from

Washington than the *Queen Mary* was accorded, the number of visitors to the ship and the loss of "souvenirs" was at least as great as the French ship had sustained'.

The issue of speed was not only a matter of pride, but also of critical financial importance, since the majority of prospective passengers buying a ticket across the Atlantic had little loyalty, caring only about the shortest length of passage. The issue had been down-played by Cunard, however, who considered it a vulgar way to measure the relative greatness of a ship. But the gloom resounding from the failure of the *Queen Mary* to break the *Normandie*'s record, in spite of Cunard's assurances that it had not even tried to do so, put an increasing amount of pressure on the company to achieve a faster run; and in August 1936, she bettered her French counterpart's record by two hours and 35 minutes, averaging 30.14 knots on a four day and 27 minute crossing between Southampton and New York. As the record alternated between the two liners, engineering adjustments were made to increase speed. As Robert Maguglin has related: 'Cunard's engineers reviewed the *Queen Mary*'s design and decided her performance could be improved with a new type of propeller. A set of 30-ton, four-bladed propellers was cast in manganese bronze. Each propeller was 18 feet in diameter. The *Queen Mary*, with her new propellers installed, finally settled her rivalry with the *Normandie* in August, 1938. She steamed to New York in three days, 21 hours and 48 minutes at an average speed of 30.99 knots (35.66 mph/57.39 kmph) and returned to England even faster in three days, 20 hours and 42 minutes at an average speed of 31.69 knots (36.47 mph/58.67 kmph).'

Buoyed up by the national excitement surrounding the event, the London *Daily Mail* chartered a special plane to meet the *Queen Mary* as she sailed homeward, and on 15 August 1938 their correspondent filed this breathless report:

'From the air yesterday I saw the *Queen Mary* tear over the last few miles that separated her from

Bishop's Rock (Scillies), then smash every speed record in Atlantic history. And early this morning she was racing up the Channel to Southampton once more holder of the proud title of the fastest liner in the world. From Ambrose Light (New York) to Bishop's Rock, the Blue Riband course, she had averaged 31.69 knots and can now claim –

The fastest westbound crossing;
The fastest eastbound crossing;
The fastest double journey; and
The fastest Atlantic day's run.

'The sight of her yesterday, majestically thrusting her vast bulk onward, was something I shall never forget. Her razor bows sent up a 20 feet eyebrow of foam perfect in its symmetry. Behind her

Below Philatelic greetings cards, recording the *Queen Mary*'s maiden sailing to New York on 27 May 1936.

boiled a creamy wake that trailed back half a mile and slowly lost itself in two creases that grew ever fainter. Her great funnels belched black smoke that remained in the sky long after she had gone and told of her passing.

'My aeroplane was the only thing on land or sea or in the sky to greet the great ship at the moment when she broke the record. In her honour we dipped and swooped round her bows and her stern, while those aboard waved to us in acknowledgement. Finding her was not easy. We were off Land's End soon after 2pm and thought to put down at the aerodrome for a spell after the run from Croydon. Our latest advice when we left was that the *Queen Mary* would pass Bishop's Rock at 4pm. Visibility was about 20 miles in the air, but there was a heat haze on the water that had made shipping more than five miles off difficult to see. So we stayed aloft and nosed gently around at 1,000 feet. At 2.30 with the Scilly Isles to starboard, pilot P H Meadway, · staring intensely ahead said: "Is it possible that

she could have got almost here by now? If so, I'll take a shade of odds that that's her." I could see nothing but a faint banner of trailing smoke above the haze on the sea. We crammed on more speed, swept down to 500 feet and kept our nose towards the leisurely twisting banner. Suddenly I saw the *Queen Mary*'s three funnels and her masts. It might have been a piece of legerdemain so swiftly and so unexpectedly did they appear. Another minute and we got the grandest view of her, head on, ripping through the flat monotony of water as scissors through a sheet. The tiny scurrying figures aboard were dwarfed in her terrific size and lost in the picture of living power that she presented.

'We came down lower, lower; and everything altered then in proportion. The *Queen Mary* dominated the sea and us and all else as we skimmed gull-like, alongside her. We were well below the level of her superstructure, turning and banking to get pictures of her. And in those few seconds I got the most vivid impression of her bulk

Below Queen Mary at sea, illustrated on the back of a folded guide to the ship issued by Cunard in 1936.

and the immense power that, unleashed, was driving her imperiously onward. Hands, hats, handkerchiefs, fluttered to us as at the moment (we judged) when she passed Bishop's Rock, we banked once more and shot the whole length of her less than 20 feet from the water's surface. I half expected a flag to be broken at her mast-head. But no. She drove on impersonally, a pride-ful gracious creature to whom, in one final dive from our bank and turn, we cried, "Well done *Queen Mary*".

The *Queen Mary* had set a dazzling new speed record, which she held for the next 14 years. Not until 1952 was her record beaten and then by the *United States*, a brand new and much lighter ship that benefitted from great advances in post-war technology. This emphasis upon speed, which had played such an important part in every aspect of the design of the *Queen Mary* from the choice of propulsion systems, fuel type and hull design at one end of the spectrum, to the thinness of wood veneers, the use of korkoid floors and other

synthetic materials for bathroom walls at the other, can be seen to run through the long series of evolutionary changes that had incrementally altered the design of ships making the Atlantic crossing. Ultimately speed was related to a profit motive reliant on increased efficiency and ever faster crossing times.

After her record-breaking run in August 1936, during which the *Queen Mary* broke the four-day barrier – the maritime equivalent of the four-minute mile – Cunard refused to accept the Hales Trophy, restating its long-established policy that safety, rather than speed, was the company's main objective. More than a mark of recognition, the Blue Riband, and the Hales Trophy that came to represent it formally, was a thinly-veiled institutionalized symbol of the starkly commercial struggle for financial survival in which shipping lines had been engaged since transatlantic service first began. This struggle became particularly explicit between the *Queen Mary* and her arch-rival the *Normandie*, partly because of the

Above A stylized illustration of the *Queen Mary* incorporated in a 1936 Cunard White Star letterhead.

historical enmity between the countries that sponsored them, but also, more significantly, because of the different philosophies that each represented.

The differences between the *Normandie* and the *Queen Mary* could not have been more pronounced, each seeming to embody the stereotyped characteristics of their respective nations. It was a question of elegance versus stateliness. While the *Queen Mary* was the product of empirical design, the result of collaboration between administrators at Cunard and engineers at John Brown's Clydebank works, the *Normandie* was borne of inspired impulse, designed by a Russian émigré named Vladimir Yourkevitch who was anything but conservative in his approach. Having only had previous experience on battleships for the Imperial Russian Navy, he followed the pattern of many of his countrymen and escaped to Paris during the Russian revolution, working for Renault before returning to naval architecture at St Nazaire. His work came to the attention of the director, André Levy, to whom he submitted drawings for a ship with a revolutionary new profile. As described by John Maxtone-Graham, this profile appeared to be: 'distressingly pear-shaped. Yet this unsightly waist provided a reserve of buoyant displacement that permitted Yourkevitch his astonishingly efficient bow. Afloat, the spread of her bilges concealed, the *Normandie* had a remarkable stance, her forward thrust assured by a beakheaded stem that terminated in a bulbous forefoot after the *Bremen*'s example. An abnormally long and fine entry at the water line, hollowed out under flaring upper strokes, reduced her bow wave to a minimum and served to neutralize flanking turbulence.'

The bow aside, other more arcane comparisons reinforce the stylistic differences between the two ships. At 1,029 feet, the *Normandie* was only 11 feet longer than her rival (although shorter at the waterline) as well as 1,774 tons lighter and one foot wider in the beam. Both had four propellers, those of the *Queen Mary* driven by geared steam-turbine drive, and the *Normandie* powered by turbo-electric propulsion. Predominantly

The *Queen Mary* makes her way up the Hudson River for the first time, heading towards her New York berth at Pier 90, accompanied by a small flotilla of welcoming craft.

fitted out in glass and metal instead of veneered wood, the *Normandie*, of the 'semi-bulbous bow' rather than raked stem and cruiser stern, was a modernist Francophilian fantasy with a first-class dining salon that looked as if it had been transplanted directly from the Champs Elysées. Electrically rather than naturally lit, it was at 46 by 305 feet, strictly rectangular rather than nearly square, with a horizontal emphasis focused on a long monumental stair, rather than on the vertical height of the space. Down this stair, as was the established tradition in great French ships, ladies performed a ritual descent, while the diners below in formal dress looked up with a critical eye. With its narrowness alleviated, directionality maintained, and its elegant occupants duplicated in walls of mirrored glass, the salon seemed to glitter, and the tall, internally-lit *jardinières* marching down each side of the long, thin room accentuated that impression. With all of the emphasis that the designers of the *Queen Mary* placed on its cabin-class restaurant and kitchens, and all of the hoopla surrounding the quantity of its provisions, the consensus of opinion on the cuisine was that it was uninspired hotel fare. The reports from the *Normandie*, however, were glowing, and many passengers signed up for the food alone, despite the liner's slower speed.

Both the *Queen Mary* and the *Normandie* were initially plagued by vibration, as well as roll, caused by the colliding effect of the waves which could typically reduce the speed of each by about two knots in rough weather. New propellers, with four blades instead of three were found to satisfactorily reduce the trembling of the *Normandie*, much to the relief of its loyal fans, but the *Queen Mary* had to wait until 1958 for stabilizers to be fitted to reduce her tendency to roll badly in storm conditions.

Storms were a regular hazard on the North Atlantic run; they would frequently whip up unexpectedly and moreover could be fierce. Evelyn Waugh in *Brideshead Revisited* describes Charles Ryder's experience of just such a storm.

From his description it is easy to locate him in the *Queen Mary*: 'The great bronze doors of the lounge had torn away from their hooks and were swinging free with the roll of the ship; regularly and, it seemed, irresistibly, first one, then the other, opened and shut; they paused at the completion of each half circle, began to move slowly and finished fast with a resounding crash. There was no real risk in passing them, except of slipping and being caught by that swift final blow...

'After luncheon ... the bronze doors of the lounge had been fixed, but not before two seamen had been badly injured. They had tried various devices, lashing with ropes and, later, when these had failed, with steel hawsers, but there was nothing to which they could be made fast; finally they drove wooden wedges under them, catching them in the brief moment of repose when they were full open and these held firm.'

Opposite page The *Queen Mary's* great rival, *Normandie*, the French Line's Blue Riband-winning liner, as depicted in a 1937 poster by Jan Auvigne.

Above A French Line poster advertising the *Normandie's* transatlantic service, with artwork by Albert Sebille.

Above right The *Normandie*'s first-class dining room, one of the most elegant and well-appointed in the world, had a distinct culinary edge over the *Queen Mary*'s restaurant.

Right A detail of the sitting room, and dining room beyond, of one of the *Normandie*'s special first-class suites.

In spite of an efficient and stylish profile, and great comfort, cuisine and service, the *Normandie* was never a profitable enterprise, and required government subsidies year after year to remain in operation. Cunard's $35,000,000 initial investment on the other hand, paid them handsome dividends, and early predictions of financial loss in the press proved to be unwarranted. The break-even passenger level, calculated in dollars by *Fortune* magazine in 1936, was based on 20 round trips a year, with one month lay-up in January, for routine maintenance. While the *Queen Mary* had a capacity of 2,100 passengers, 'full', due to average disposition in all the cabins, which were not booked by the numbers they were designated to hold, was considered by Cunard to be 1,900. Outgoing costs were formidable. Fuel, as the most obvious of these, was consumed at a rate of 11,000 tons per round trip which, at $7.26 a ton, cost $80,000; and more in rough weather when consumption increased. Wages, for a crew of 1,050, totalled $35,000. Food costs were $3.00 a day for a cabin-class passenger, $2.60 in tourist and $1.00 for third class. Mainte-

Cassandre's famous poster of the *Normandie*, used for the French Line's advertising campaigns throughout the 1930s, reveals the sweeping lines and stream-lined simplicity of this most elegant of ships.

The brand new *Queen Mary* steaming at full speed, sending a plume of spray up at her bows and leaving a wide foaming wake behind her. From August 1938 when she finally took the Atlantic record from the *Normandie*, until the launch of the *United States* in 1952, the *Queen Mary* was the fastest ocean liner in the world and the unchallenged holder of the coveted Blue Riband.

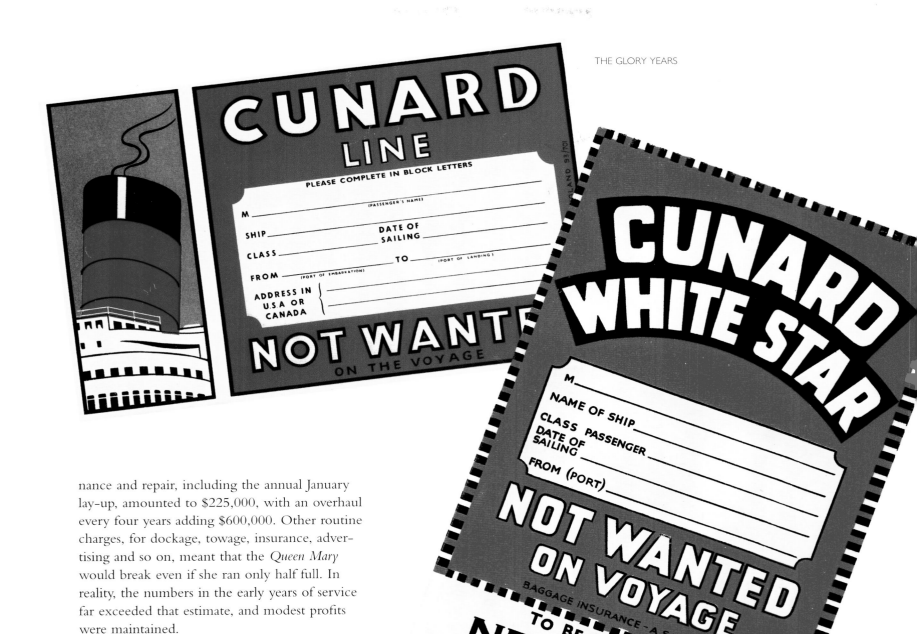

CUNARD
LINE

PLEASE COMPLETE IN BLOCK LETTERS

(PASSENGER'S NAME)

M

SHIP   DATE OF
                              SAILING

CLASS   TO   (PORT OF LANDING)

FROM   (PORT OF EMBARKATION)

ADDRESS IN
U.S.A OR
CANADA

NOT WANTE
ON THE VOYAGE

CUNARD
WHITE STAR

M

NAME OF SHIP

CLASS PASSENGER

DATE OF
SAILING

FROM (PORT)

NOT WANTED
ON VOYAGE

BAGGAGE INSURANCE – A SAFE POLICY

TO BE LANDED AT
NEW YORK

PRINTED IN ENGLAND

nance and repair, including the annual January lay-up, amounted to $225,000, with an overhaul every four years adding $600,000. Other routine charges, for dockage, towage, insurance, advertising and so on, meant that the *Queen Mary* would break even if she ran only half full. In reality, the numbers in the early years of service far exceeded that estimate, and modest profits were maintained.

But, on a darker note, as the *Queen Mary* set out on her maiden voyage the clouds of war were already forming. Ominously, as she arrived in Southampton water for the first time, the *Queen Mary* had passed the outward-bound liner *Bremen*, a former Blue Riband holder. Although she signalled a friendly greeting, those on board the new ship could not have missed the Nazi swastika flying from the German liner's mast. Between the suspension of work on job number *534* in December 1931 and the beginning of commercial service five years later, Adolf Hitler had been appointed Chancellor in Germany, and had abandoned the League of Nations and begun to rearm. In spite of the fact that a new Palais de Nations was built in 1936, this institution was to

prove powerless in stopping the rapid succession of events that would soon follow on the road to an international conflagration. The war, which was seen as an increasing possibility through 1937 and 1938, would soon make calculations of the *Queen Mary*'s economic potential purely academic, as this paragon of luxury was destined for much more mundane use – as a troopship *par excellence*.

Above Cunard baggage labels dating from the 1930s.

As the *Queen Mary* set out from Southampton with 2,332 passengers aboard on 30 August 1939, little more than three years and five months after her maiden voyage, few had

The *Queen Mary* as nursery at war's end: a GI bride and her charges.

foreseen that Great Britain

HOLDING THE LINE !

Winston Churchill as a 'British bulldog' holds the line; Churchill made several Atlantic crossings on the *Queen Mary* during the war and set in train the preparations for the D-day landings while on board.

would be at war with Germany before she reached the other side of the Atlantic. Suddenly, mid-way into her last commercial voyage for more than seven years, the ship that had come to epitomize the style and elegance of the thirties, was at risk of attack by enemy submarines.

Opposite The *Queen Mary* escorted by a British Navy cruiser, HMS *Scylla*. Soon after the outbreak of war the *Queen*

Mary was called up for military service, given a uniform coat of battleship-grey paint and set in service as a troopship.

Right Servicemen boarding the *Queen Mary* were given badges in one of three colours denoting their section of the ship.

Above A unique line-up; the three largest liners in the world, the *Normandie*, *Queen Mary* and the newly-arrived *Queen Elizabeth*, tied up at piers 88 and 90 in New York in March 1940. The two British ships would soon leave on war service, while the French liner remained moth-balled, awaiting a US Govern-ment decision on her fate.

Right 'Passengers' boarding the *Queen Mary* during her time as a troopship were issued this card, politely asking them not to show a light or smoke on the outside decks after dark, which might compromise the ship's strict blackout observance.

The majority of the record number of passengers on board the *Queen Mary* on that August voyage, had feared that hostilities in Europe might break out shortly and, like many before them, they had taken the opportunity to return to America while it was still possible to do so. As soon as war was declared, on 3 September 1939, cancelled sailings turned the piers at Southampton into chaos, especially since the Germans almost immediately made their intentions towards what they considered to be 'belligerent ships' clear by sending the Cunarder *Athenia* to the bottom of the ocean off the north coast of Ireland with two torpedoes to the hull. The plight of the *Aquitania* which was set to sail on the day that war was declared, and left on schedule is indicative of this confusion. When the posters went up, confirming that the ship would make the crossing regardless of hostilities, there was a frisson of panic at Southampton. In a statement worded almost exactly like that read to the passengers of the ill-fated *Lusitania*, which had been sunk during World War I as she passed the Old Head of Kinsale off the Irish coast on 8 May 1915, on her way to Liverpool, a Consular officer read out a warning: 'American citizens are hereby advised that they are taking passage on a belligerent ship and are subject to sinking without notice.'

The *Queen Mary*, with portholes blacked out and sailing at top speed, arrived safely at New York and remained at Pier 90 on the Hudson River throughout the winter of 1939, while the so-called 'Phoney War' was acted out in Europe. The *Normandie* took up residence nearby, at Pier 88, shortly afterwards. But while the *Normandie* remained resplendent in her peace-time livery, the *Queen Mary* suffered the almost immediate indignity of being painted from stem to stern with a coat of anonymous battle-ship grey. Six months later, early in March 1940, the prematurely-launched *Queen Elizabeth* unexpectedly appeared through the grey gloom of the late winter after-noon, to join the other two great liners. Having decided that the likelihood of enemy attack was too risky in its fitting-out basin at Clydebank, the British Government ordered the date of comple-tion of the *Queen Elizabeth* to be moved forward substantially, and under the guise of 'sea trials' sent her speeding across the Atlantic, out of harm's way. For the last two weeks of March 1940, New Yorkers had the opportunity to compare the *Queen Mary*, *Queen Elizabeth* and *Normandie* resting side by side in their berths for the first and last time.

To the *New York Post* the *Queen Elizabeth* appeared like 'an Empress incognito, gray-veiled for her desperate exploit'. As Maxtone-Graham describes the scene of her arrival: 'By the time she reached her berth in late afternoon, thousands of office and shore-front workers thronged the West Side to cheer the newest Queen. If she was scarcely dressed for the occasion, the brilliance of her escape from the Germans gave the moment a particular drama all its own. That vast, sombre ship, nudged deli-

R.M.S. "QUEEN MARY"

As a purely precautionary measure, all passengers are forbidden to smoke, strike matches, or show any kind of light on any of the outside decks between sunset and sunrise. Passengers are also requested to use the outer decks as little as possible during darkness, and are for-bidden to use the Sun Deck during the aforementioned hours. The Commodore requests that all passengers will co-operate with the foregoing instructions.

Left 'She Talked … This Happened'; a poster from the 'Careless Talk Costs Lives' campaign, issued by the British Government during the war, with artwork by Abram Games. The safety of the *Queen Mary* at sea was a constant concern, and her itinerary was a well-kept secret, known only to the captain and senior officers.

cately into the slip just north of her sister, gave symbolic presence to the war that America was yet to enter.'

On 1 March 1940, Cunard was informed by the Admiralty that the *Queen Mary* and her sister were being requisitioned for military service. By mid-March, a fresh coat of grey paint had been applied to the *Queen Mary*'s hull and superstructure, and 500 personnel were transferred from the *Antonia* soon afterwards. Many interior fittings were also removed, and packed into the hold for final storage in Sydney where, in the incredibly short time of 18 days, between 17 April and 5 May 1940, the *Queen Mary* was equipped with armaments and refitted to meet the carrying requirements of its intended 5,000 troops. No time was lost in utilizing this new capability, as missions involving the transport of a full complement of Australian troops, from Sydney to Greenock, took place on 6 May, and of British troops to Suez soon after.

During her years of military service the *Queen Mary*, together with the *Queen Elizabeth*, transported thousands of troops to and from the arenas of war. Between them, the liners had a carrying capacity of up to 15,000 men – the best part of

Opposite On 21 March 1940 the *Queen Mary* took leave of her neighbour the *Normandie* and backed away from her New York berth, thus beginning her war service after months of inactivity. Bound for 'an unknown destination', she steamed first to Cape Town and then to Sydney, Australia, where her remaining furnishings and fittings were removed and her conversion to a troopship was completed.

Above 'The *Queen Mary* Raising Steam', by Norman Wilkinson; painted in a battleship grey, the ship prepares to leave Gourock on another secret voyage.

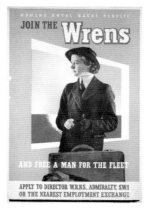

a division – and in the summer entire regiments slept on deck. Many of the crossings were between New York and Gourock, the *Queen Mary*'s wartime Scottish port. American troops brought by the liners were sent to orientation camps in England before being dispersed to the battlefields of Europe, Asia and North Africa.

Troops were not the only passengers, however. In May 1943 the *Queen Mary* was requisitioned to take a delegation including the British Prime Minister Winston Churchill, Lord Beaverbrook and Field Marshal Wavell, with a staff of officers and clerks, to meet strategists in New York. Doctors had advised the Prime Minister against travelling by air so soon after a bout of pneumonia, and the *Queen Mary* was chosen for her speed. A diary written at the time by Field Marshal Viscount Alanbrooke recounts how preparatory discussions revolved around both security during the trip and an infestation of insects, believed to have been caused by coolies unloading equipment during the liner's run from Australia to Suez:

'We were told about the vermin which had resulted from troop movements. It was impossible to clear this entirely without going into dry-dock and a long process, but by a system of gassing, the live insects would be killed but not their eggs. We should consequently have the period of incubation, about six days, of relative immunity. PM accepted the risk. The last blow however was a heavier one. The ship was "dry"! At this Winston pulled a very long face, but was reassured that the suite occupied by him need not be ...'

Security for the voyage relied on a system of convoys and naval escorts. After fitting-out especially for the trip, the *Queen Mary* set sail at 5.30pm from Greenock, Scotland. Alanbrooke recorded his first impressions of the transformed liner:

'We arrived at Greenock at 3.40pm and then transferred to a launch which took us to the *Queen Mary*. The height of her was most impressive as we drew alongside, and when we got on board it was a job to find one's way about. She

Opposite top War service introduced many incongruous new activities into the *Queen Mary*'s rooms; here the tourist-class playroom serves as the Royal Air Force's orderly room.

Opposite left Furniture in the main lounge under protective shrouds.

Opposite right The cabin-class restaurant lined with mess-room galley tables.

Above left The tourist-class cocktail bar on main deck pressed into use as a pharmacy.

Above right A wartime recruitment poster, urging women to join the Wrens (Women's Royal Naval Service). During the war Wrens staffed the *Queen Mary*'s Communications Office and performed other important duties on board.

Above The *Queen Mary* ploughs full steam ahead through a North Atlantic swell, sending a huge wave breaking over her bridge. Her remarkable speed, faster than any naval warship, allowed the *Queen Mary* to outrun danger; her tendency to hove into view and then almost immediately vanish, earned her the nickname, the 'Grey Ghost'.

had been completely stripped and turned into a troop carrier, and it has entailed considerable work restoring her into a suitable condition to take the PM and us. They have done marvels in the short time and the cabin I am in must be up to pre-war standard. A very large double room very well fitted with sitting-room, two bathrooms and masses of cupboards and armchairs, etc.'

The main deck had been transformed into a series of offices, conference rooms and a map room for ship-board work by the delegation. About 5,000 German prisoners were also aboard, sealed off from the rest of the passengers. The journey was made successfully, but under constant threat of attack. Alanbrooke's entry in his diary as the ship neared New York conveys something of the ordeal that the ship's crew had undergone while their charges had been discussing strategies for bringing the war to a close:

'May 10th. *Queen Mary*. This should be our last day at sea, as we are due to arrive tomorrow

morning if we go on defeating submarines as we have up to the present. There are about a hundred of them operating in the North Atlantic, but most of them are concentrated further north. There are only two reported in front of us on the approaches to New York. But as we have now also picked up a Catalina flying-boat in addition to our two cruisers and four destroyers, we should be well protected.'

During her military service the *Queen Mary* escaped serious damage, a remarkable fact at a time when U-boats posed a threat by day and by night. Having entered the war with 57 submarines, Germany had built more than a thousand by 1945. During the war's longest battle – that of the Atlantic – between 1939 and 1945, 2,828 ships were sunk. As the historian Leslie Reade has pointed out: 'The almost incredible fact was, that in over five years of war service, having sailed hundreds of thousands of miles in most of the oceans of the world, and carried the better part of a million of military and other

Above Wartime exercises on the sun deck.

Left Officers dining in the tourist-class dining saloon which appears to have retained at least some of its pre-war dignity.

Overleaf 'Action Stations' sends gunners running to two anti-aircraft gun emplacements erected on the cabin-class games deck aft of the verandah grill.

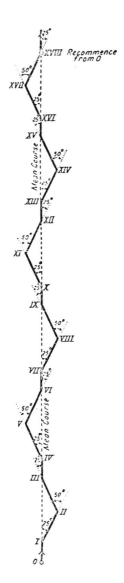

passengers, the *Queen Mary* never saw a submarine, never was fired on from the air or from the sea or the land, never had a bomb dropped on her, and, on her own account, never fired a shot in anger.'

Much of that enviable record was due to her speed which, in excess of 30 knots, or 34.5 mph, was faster than enemy torpedoes – in the early stages of the war, at least. Voyages were navigated on ever-changing, zig-zagging routes and sonar detection devices were installed to help the ship to avoid enemy submarines. This, together with her camouflage covering, soon earned the *Queen Mary* the nickname of the 'Grey Ghost'. Stories of her elusive appearances and disappearances through fog and mist, by other ships at sea have now entered the realm of maritime legend.

Her war service was not without mishap, however. On 27 September 1942, the *Queen Mary* sailed from New York with a remarkable 10,398 American troops on board, en route to Scotland. It was customary for an escort to meet the liner in coastal waters, and on Friday 2 October 1942 the captain, Commodore Sir Gordon Illingworth, sighted the light cruiser HMS *Curacoa* which, along with six destroyers, had been assigned to provide anti-submarine protection onwards into Gourock. At the time of the encounter, the *Queen Mary*, steaming at 28.5 knots, was on an evasive course, known as Zig-Zag No 8, its chief defence against torpedoes in open water, which required frequent, alternating turns across its mean course of 106 degrees. Running four knots slower than its charge, the *Curacoa* had no chance of keeping ahead, but was well in front of the protective convoy when, at 1.30pm, in clear weather, the bow of the *Queen Mary* hit the ship on its port side, slightly aft of the middle of the 450-feet-long hull, cutting it completely in two. The *Curacoa* sank within five minutes and 329 of its 430 crew members were killed. Weighing the risk to the thousands of troops in his care that stopping to lower lifeboats for survivors would have entailed in those especially treacherous

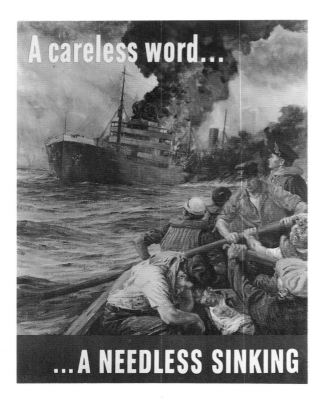

A careless word...

...A NEEDLESS SINKING

waters, the captain made the only possible decision, to continue on course, leaving rescue efforts to the destroyers astern. At the time of impact, Captain Illingworth was in the charthouse, and had just asked his Junior First and Navigating Officer to send for the signalman to signal an estimated time of arrival. Feeling, but not being able to see the collision, he feared that the ship had been hit by a bomb. In contrast to the *Curacoa*, the damage to the *Queen Mary* was relatively minor, confined to a long vertical gash on the prow. Fortunately, this was sealed by the steel plates that had wrapped over it under the force of the collision. The first watertight collision bulkhead held and the ship, proceeding cautiously at 13.5 knots, arrived at the Clyde unassisted.

In the hearings that followed, the Commissioners for Executing the Office of Lord High Admiral of the United Kingdom, who had filed suit against Cunard White Star Ltd, claiming compensation for the loss of the cruiser, took the position that the *Queen Mary* did not follow its zig-zag pattern exactly, and should have

Above American servicemen crowded on the *Queen Mary*'s sun deck.

Right GIs milling around in the *Queen Mary*'s main hall and shopping centre on the promenade deck.

turned to port sooner than it did. It also blamed the *Queen Mary*'s look-out for carelessness. A judgment based primarily on precedents established in the Articles of the Regulations for Preventing Collisions at Sea, as well as eye-witness testimony, was passed on 21 January 1947, and held that the *Curacoa* was entirely to blame, and should have taken greater care to steer clear of its charge. The Admiralty appealed, and under re-examination, the look-out on the *Queen Mary* was also held responsible. On 30 July 1947, a second judgment reapportioned blame as belonging one-third to the *Queen Mary* and

two-thirds to the *Curacoa*, a decision that was upheld under subsequent appeal.

Following temporary repairs and reinforcement of the bow and collision bulkhead in Gourock, during which several tons of cement were poured into the ridge of the bow to seal it, the *Queen Mary* sailed to dry dock in the Boston Navy Yard, at a reduced speed of 21 knots, for final repairs. News of the accident was suppressed, on the grounds that the incident could have been used for propaganda purposes; but, in retrospect, the blackout was more effective in Britain than in

Above The *Queen Mary* loaded with as many men as she could possibly carry. Crowding such as this caused great discomfort, particularly when sailing in warmer climates, and there were many wartime deaths on board.

great liners, among them the *Ile de France*, the *Nieuw Amsterdam*, the *Queen of Bermuda*, and her fellow Cunarder, the *Aquitania*. It was one of the most dangerous events in her military career. Captain Bisset, as commodore of the convoy, described it in his journal as 'the most anxious voyage that I made in the *Queen Mary*, and the biggest responsibility that I have ever had thrust upon me'. The convoy had been charged with returning the Australian expeditionary force of over 31,000 troops to their own nation, then under threat of invasion by the Japanese. The order was that all the ships in the convoy should stay together, and the *Queen Mary* was therefore restricted to the speed of the slowest member of the group, the *Queen of Bermuda*, whose top speed was only 18 knots. With one third of the entire expeditionary force on board, and a bounty on her equivalent to a quarter of a million dollars, plus the prospect of being decorated by Adolf Hitler, submarine commanders would most certainly have chosen the *Queen Mary* out of the entire convoy as the most attractive target, and Captain Bisset knew it. Having participated as a junior officer in the *Carpathia*'s rescue of the

Above Wartime posters, with artwork by Abram Games, exhorting Britons to grow their own food and relieve the pressure on the Atlantic convoys, and urging them to economize and save lives during the Battle of the Atlantic.

Right Berthing cards issued to servicemen embarking on the *Queen Mary*.

Opposite above GIs relieve the boredom of life on board with a game of poker. Standee berths such as these were fitted in every part of the ship. A cabin-class stateroom, designed for two passengers, could accommodate 21 men sleeping barely 18 inches apart.

Opposite left Some of the worst living conditions on board were to be found in the cabin-class swimming pool where berths were stacked seven high. Here the bunks are aired in readiness for the next wave of servicemen.

Opposite right The ship's sickbay.

Germany, and the real motive behind the silence surrounding the affair seems to have been the demoralizing effect it would have had on the Royal Navy.

Following this tragic accident, which was effectively kept secret until the end of the war, the *Queen Mary* regularly transported more American troops to Gourock, and in December 1942 embarked from New York on what became known as 'the long voyage'. It lasted more than six months and involved stops at Gourock, Freetown, Capetown, Aden, Suez, and on to Sydney, then back to Gourock and, finally, to New York where she berthed at Pier 90 on 16 June 1943. Along the way the *Queen Mary* had covered more than 46,000 miles and carried 45,000 passengers, all without incident.

The ship was commanded on this voyage by Captain Bisset, who became the *Queen Mary*'s post-war commodore. After disembarking 10,000 allied troops at Suez she left on 25 January as part of an extraordinary convoy of some of the world's

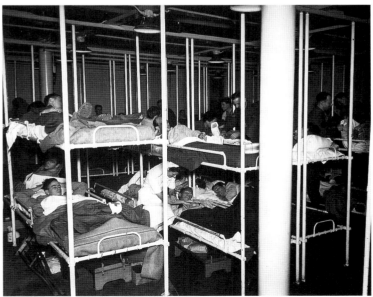

Right The *Queen Mary* at anchor off Capetown early in 1940.

Opposite A US Navy blimp and coastguard vessels greet the *Queen Mary* as she nears New York on 20 June 1945, bringing home the first wave of victorious American troops.

survivors of the sinking of the *Titanic*, he was no stranger to the perils of the sea, and fully realized that without its one great advantage of speed, his ship was at grave risk. But his only recourse was to comply with his orders, remain in the convoy and trust to luck, which fortunately held.

The demand for more and more troops, as the war ground on, put an ever-increasing burden on the *Queen Mary*'s capacity as a carrier, as constant refits continued to allow more passengers. Six months after leading the perilous convoy to Australia, additional standee berths were added, making stacks of six with only a foot and a half between them. Three men sleeping in shifts were assigned to each berth, with thousands of others relegated to sleeping on deck. A rotation system allowed those below to switch with those on deck twice during the Atlantic crossing. The ship was also zoned to restrict movement, which made life aboard a bit easier. Buttons in one of three colours, corresponding to red, white and blue zones, were issued on embarkation, alleviating

the strain on sanitary systems and load distribution, and making it possible to unload off Gourock efficiently. Meals were also served by rotation, with each soldier receiving two meals a day, at breakfast and suppertime. This required the kitchen, where staff also served in shifts, to be in operation 24 hours a day to meet the demand.

In these crowded quarters, in which, for example, a cabin-class stateroom, originally designed to accommodate two passengers, had been converted to hold 21, conditions were uncomfortable enough, but on tropical runs, especially in the lower decks where air-conditioning had not been installed, they were appalling. As Leslie Reade has said: 'In such over-crowding of human beings it is possible there had been no parallel since the infamous slavers of an earlier age. The essential difference, of course, was that the slavers were packed with cruelty and without intelligence and the giant steamers with a sensitive understanding of the limits of human

tolerance and a meticulous knowledge of household economy on a colossal scale afloat.'

Like the passengers on the slave ships, some men also died as a result of overheating and suffocation. Following service in returning the Australian expeditionary force for the defence of its homeland, however, the tropical voyages ended, and the North Atlantic run was continued. It was upon resumption of this familiar route that the *Queen Mary* set the record for the greatest number of passengers that have ever sailed in one ship, carrying 15,740 troops and 943 staff, a total of 16,683 persons, which has yet to be equalled. Her capacity to deliver an entire division to the opposite side of the Atlantic in five days, had been cited by Winston Churchill as a critical factor in shortening the war. Churchill continued to travel on the *Queen Mary* during the course of the conflict, and afterwards. Using the code name Colonel Warden, he sailed to the Quadrant and Octagon war conferences in August 1943 and September 1944 respectively, using his suite as a command post in which he first reviewed the plans for the D-Day invasion.

Towards the end of the war the *Queen Mary* also bore the brunt of the results of her efficiency as

Opposite Almost every inch of deck space is crowded with returning servicemen eager for a first glimpse of Manhattan and the crowds on the quayside.

Above The *Queen Mary* heads up the Hudson River on the afternoon of 20 June 1945 bound for Pier 90 and one of the warmest welcomes of her career.

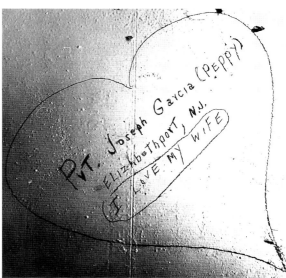

a troop transport, serving as a hospital ship on which the wounded were returned to the United States, as were the first victorious United States units one month after VE Day on 8 May 1945. They were followed by numerous GI brides and their children travelling to be reunited with the hundreds of thousands of Yanks that she had originally delivered to England, 'over-paid, over-sexed and over here'. This last was perhaps the most uncharacteristic and unlikely role of all, as this effective instrument of war was quickly transformed into a floating nursery. Thirteen voyages were scheduled to permit more than 20,000 women and children to rejoin their husbands. The sun and promenade decks that had once been stylish floating boulevards on which passengers strolled, or sat in cosseted warmth on blanket-wrapped deck chairs, and had more recently been crammed with thousands of soldiers on their way to the battlefield, now looked like Sunday in Hyde Park, with babies in perambulators being rapidly wheeled ahead of a stiff mid-Atlantic breeze. Cabin-class suites were quickly converted to nurseries, and the surgery also served a new purpose as a delivery room for the four babies born at sea over the course of these voyages.

Finally, having delivered a last load of women and children to eager husbands in Canada and the United States, the *Queen Mary* was demobilized on 29 September 1946 and was free to return to Southampton. Refitting her for commercial service would take ten months. A battalion of 1,500 men from John Brown's yard on the Clyde had come down to work on the ship at the Thorneycroft works in Southampton, camping in temporary accommodation nearby. In dry dock the *Queen Mary*'s propellers would be overhauled, the shafts drawn out for inspection and the paraphernalia of her wartime service including bunks, armour, gun emplacements, and mine-repelling equipment removed. As she arrived in Southampton, her funnels already repainted in the familiar Cunard red, she was greeted as a defiant symbol of national pride and vision, a survivor of the perils of war, ready to enter a new era of prosperity and stability.

Scenes on board the *Queen Mary* from her 13 voyages transporting war brides and children. She made the first of these in February 1946 and went on to carry more than 22,000 women and children to the United States and Canada where they were reunited with husbands and fathers. For most of these women, their first sight of the United States was from the *Queen Mary*'s deck rail.

Overleaf The *Queen Mary* receives a jubilant welcome as she returns to Southampton on 27 September 1946, concluding her last voyage as a troop carrier.

The *Queen Mary* was finally demobilized on 29 September 1946. By that time she had spent more than half of her working life as a troopship, her red Cunard livery obscured beneath a drab coat of military grey. Her refurbishment brought her back to life. Modernized, and ready to re-enter transatlantic service, she immediately regained her pre-war following, attracting celebrities, film stars and royalty to her elegant staterooms. A passage on the *Queen Mary* was, once again, the only way to cross.

As a potent symbol of gracious living, the *Queen Mary* was always a magnet for the rich and famous. Here British actor Rex Harrison and his wife pose for the ship's photographer on the sun deck.

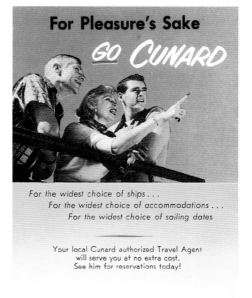

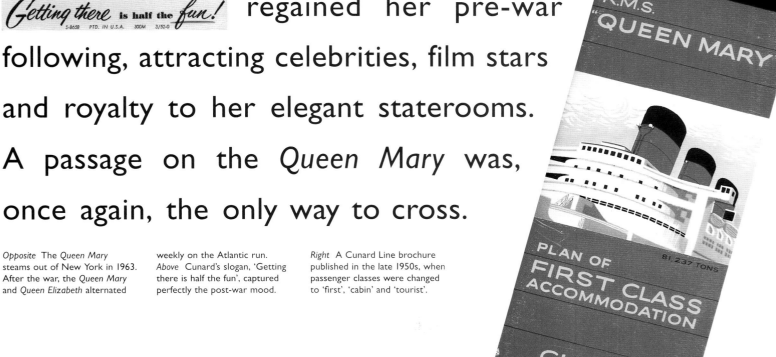

Opposite The *Queen Mary* steams out of New York in 1963. After the war, the *Queen Mary* and *Queen Elizabeth* alternated weekly on the Atlantic run. *Above* Cunard's slogan, 'Getting there is half the fun', captured perfectly the post-war mood. *Right* A Cunard Line brochure published in the late 1950s, when passenger classes were changed to 'first', 'cabin' and 'tourist'.

The war over, the *Queen Mary* arrived in her home port of Southampton, for yet another metamorphosis. The task ahead was overwhelming, amounting to nothing less than the complete refurbishment of the interior of the ship, and substantial alterations to the exterior. While the anonymous wartime grey paint was obscured, furniture, divided between store rooms in Sydney and New York, and which amounted to more than ten thousand pieces, was slowly reassembled and a small army of construction workers prepared the public rooms and cabins to receive them.

The shipyard workers that came aboard the *Queen Mary* at Southampton found that every part of the ship had been converted to purposes quite different to those originally intended, as berths were inserted into every available square inch of space. Bunks had been stacked seven tiers high in the cabin-class swimming pool and cafeteria-style tables and benches were screwed to the floor of the main dining salon; the tourist-class children's playroom had been transformed into an orderly room for the RAF, and the tourist-class bar on the main deck had taken on an unlikely role as a pharmacy; teak railings on the sports, sun, promenade and main decks had been carved with the initials of thousands of

Opposite The *Queen Mary* returns to Southampton after her demobilization from wartime service. On her way to dry dock she passes the *Queen Elizabeth*, newly refitted and ready for her long-postponed maiden commercial voyage.

Below A Cunard baggage label depicting the *Queen Elizabeth*.

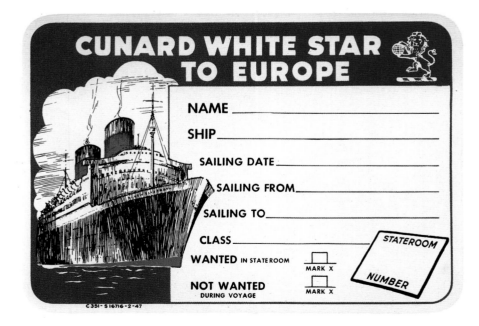

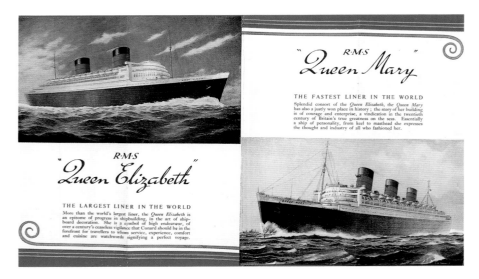

RMS "Queen Mary"

THE FASTEST LINER IN THE WORLD

Splendid consort of the *Queen Elizabeth*, the *Queen Mary* has also a justly won place in history ; the story of her building is of courage and enterprise, a vindication in the twentieth century of Britain's true greatness on the seas. Essentially a ship of personality, from keel to masthead she expresses the thought and industry of all who fashioned her.

RMS "Queen Elizabeth"

THE LARGEST LINER IN THE WORLD

More than the world's largest liner, the *Queen Elizabeth* is an epitome of progress in shipbuilding, in the art of shipboard decoration. She is a symbol of high endeavour, of over a century's ceaseless vigilance that Cunard should be in the forefront for travellers to whom service, experience, comfort and cuisine are watchwords signifying a perfect voyage.

Above Cunard chose to characterize the *Queen Mary* as the world's fastest liner, and the *Queen Elizabeth* as the world's largest; the speed of the newer ship was never tested to the full, or an attempt made to capture the Blue Riband.

soldiers and their loved ones during transport. Given the complete nature of the refit that was required, Cunard decided that this was an ideal time to introduce several new features to the ship, involving improved amenities for passengers in all classes, new air-conditioned public rooms, and increased space for the crew, that would make the *Queen Mary* more commercially viable as she resumed service in the face of a changing market and new social values. For example, a new cinema replaced the starboard gallery, a cocktail bar was installed in the entrance to the cabin-class restaurant and the cabin-class gymnasium was moved to amidships on the sun deck.

The most substantial changes were made on the promenade deck; before they were implemented, however, extensive efforts were made to return the most popular rooms on that level to their pre-war glory, but with several significant alterations. The cabin-class lounge was restored and a russet and gold carpet, designed by Agnes Pinder-Davis, added to accentuate the warm brown hue of the room's high maple columns. Further forward, the observation lounge and cocktail bar, which had proven to be a favourite gathering place before the war, was now carefully reinstated, with bright red and beige curtains substituted to match more closely the original red-upholstered furniture, and tone in with the red lights behind the bar. The oval drawing room adjacent to it, was also refurbished in its original

grey-blue palette. Aft on the promenade deck, in the verandah grill, Doris Zinkeisen was recalled to restore her mural of marionettes, ballet dancers and circus performers, and asked to add a more up-to-date theme of vaguely familiar film stars, surrounded by arc lights and production crew, facing a camera, ostensibly to appeal to the celebrities that Cunard sought to attract in cabin class.

Over and above this reconditioning programme, new construction was ordered to modernize the facilities on the promenade deck and to create new enclosed areas for sitting and refreshment that could take advantage of the light and view. These new 'garden lounges' located next to the cabin-class smoking room echoed those on the *Queen Mary*'s sister ship the *Queen Elizabeth*, and were intended to equalize their appeal. Cabin-class passengers were directed to the garden lounge on the port side, while the garden lounge on the starboard side was linked to a new 'mermaid cocktail bar' and the tourist class entrance to the cinema.

The long gallery on the port side of the promenade deck, originally intended as overflow space from the cabin-class ballroom, connecting it to the clubby smoking room, came in for special attention in the renovation, possibly due to its large size and nebulous function. The paintings 'Sussex Landscape' by Bertram Nicholls and 'Evening on the Avon' by Algernon Newton were removed from their protective casings and retained, and augmented by a carved frieze of pear and sycamore by Bainbridge Copnall, who had earlier contributed the series of panels in the main restaurant themed on 'Ships Throughout the Ages'. His commission for 21 vignettes of hunting scenes confirmed Cunard's continuing belief in the 'ship of beautiful woods' approach and their determination to improve on it. With its linear axis interrupted by three new wooden screens, dividing it into four distinct bays, including a 'sitting out alcove' extending into the promenade deck, the long gallery now reflected the less formal and ceremonial mood of the time, as well as the heightened desire for privacy.

In response to an equally strong requirement for less circumscribed places for dancing, the ballroom was removed, part of its floor area now disappearing into the new cinema that replaced the starboard gallery. The new 'salon' that replaced the ballroom opened directly into the long gallery, allowing the space to be treated as one room. The salon could accommodate an orchestra at its starboard end, and had room for a small dancefloor and informal seated groups. Anna Zinkeisen was recalled by Cunard for the refit and asked to provide two new panels for the salon to echo her originals. These were each to be 25 feet long and eight feet high, and were formed around the idea of 'The Chase' and 'Hunting Through the Ages', to tie in with the carvings by Bainbridge Copnall; they were also presented as being complementary to the new peach-tinted mirrors with white sycamore frames that surrounded them. The Cunard press release announcing the new paintings managed to capture the populist generality of such art: 'They have been executed with an eye to the room's primary function of dancing. "The Chase" is a vivid composition of hunting scenes merged with underwater revelry in the realm of Neptune. Mermaids in scarlet hunting jackets spur their sea horses over the crests of plumy billows, whilst Britannia, a resplendent figure in white and gold, a French horn to her lips, occupies the central scene. Numerous sea symbols, an anchor, fish and delicately coloured sea anemones complete this very arresting canvas. Above the central recess the panel shows the midday sun flanked by the figures of Justice holding her scales and Father Neptune in a festive mood.' The limited success of this new arrangement can perhaps be measured by the fact that the salon was converted to a shop during the *Queen Mary*'s 1953 winter overhaul. The long gallery became the 'midships bar' in 1963, the sitting-out alcove becoming the site for the bar.

In a limited attempt to balance the continuing use of veneer, and any old-fashioned associations that it may have conveyed, the starboard gallery was converted into a cinema using plastic as the primary decorative material. To emphasize its cold, prismatic quality a colour scheme of pastel grey and blue replaced the earth tones that had been used in the original room; indeed, the self-contained character of the space made this possible, without disrupting the continuing campaign to emphasize wood elsewhere.

The unfortunate substitution of fluorescent for incandescent lights in the garden lounges was indicative of the decorative schizophrenia involved in this renovation. It continued in the remodelled 'Regent Street' shopping arcade, which was more consciously commercial than its predecessor. In this instance the fluorescent lights tended to wash out rather than complement the custom-made wooden showcases and mast-like columns, as well as the newly-laid light brown korkoid floor. The dilemma that the designers faced, of trying to retain the aura of pre-war elegance that had made the ship so famous, while implementing minimal, yet visually effective attempts at modernization to match the standard set by her partner the

Below A Cunard embarkation notice for the Southampton–New York service depicting the *Queen Elizabeth* against the Manhattan skyline.

Above The *Queen Mary* passes her sister the *Queen Elizabeth* in mid-Atlantic. It was customary on these occasions for the ships' captains to let their two liners pass as closely as possible in order to extract the maximum drama from the encounter.

Queen Elizabeth, prompted such renovation, which was not always entirely successful.

Being newer and more modern than the *Queen Mary*, the *Queen Elizabeth* had measurably more post-war 'dash'. At 83,678 tons, she was 2,904 tons heavier than her predecessor; and with a longer profile and two widely-spaced funnels instead of three, cut a slightly more rakish figure in the water. In this respect the *Queen Elizabeth* approximated the outline of the famous Norddeutscher Lloyd Liner *Bremen*, which had successfully challenged the *Mauretania* for the Blue Riband before the war. Like the *Queen Mary*, the *Queen Elizabeth* was renovated in Southampton and took up the business of carrying passengers across the North Atlantic, on 16 October 1946. This was officially designated her maiden voyage, as she had not really had one at the start of the

war. The intervening months between this voyage and the return of the *Queen Mary* to service on 31 July 1947, were viewed as a time for testing passenger reactions to features that had been incorporated in the *Queen Elizabeth*, in order to determine whether they should be installed in the *Queen Mary* as well. One such feature was the addition of an air-conditioned cocktail bar near the *Queen Mary*'s main restaurant. Called the 'Island Bar', this rendezvous was promoted as: 'the kind of intimate meeting place that has proved to be such a great success in the *Queen Elizabeth*'. It was finished in sycamore panelling with pale white-leather banquettes and the same peach-tinted mirrors used by Anna Zinkeisen's new dance spot at the ballroom entrance to the long gallery. It pointed again to an awareness of the fickleness of public taste, and a determination to remain ahead of it.

"QUEEN MARY" "QUEEN ELIZABETH"
Fastest Ocean Service in the World

CUNARD
WHITE STAR

Ten months after arriving at Southampton for refurbishment, all of the casings protecting the wood panelling and artwork had been removed, as had the second set of extensive partitions erected as hoarding while additions were made, and new commissions were carried out. With chewing-gum-encrusted decking raised, removed or replaced, new railings in place, and furniture, carpets and curtains returned, the *Queen Mary* set out on her first commercial voyage since 30 August 1939, almost exactly eight years before. With both of the Queens now back in service, alternating like clockwork between Southampton and New York, Cunard's original mandate, of a safe, dependable weekly transatlantic ferry maintained by two ships, was realized. Furthermore, their availability in the years prior to 1950, coincided exactly with a period of expansive indulgence in the United States after years

Above The *Queen Mary* bound for New York as the *Queen Elizabeth* steams eastward towards the Atlantic. This was a rare encounter; it was more common for the two ships to pass at sea.

Left A Cunard White Star poster, with artwork by Walter Thomas, advertising the 'Fastest Ocean Service in the World'.

Above During her post-war refit, the *Queen Mary* benefitted from the experience that Cunard had gained in fitting out the *Queen Elizabeth* and from passengers' responses to the new ship. As a result, two 'garden lounges' were built on either side of the cabin-class smoking room and many other internal modifications were incorporated.

Left The 'Mermaid Cocktail Bar' located on the promenade deck between the tourist-class garden lounge, and a new purpose-built cinema, were installed in the space previously occupied by the starboard gallery.

Opposite page The cabin-class smoking room, restored to its pre-war glory but minus James Woodford's ornate bronze light sconces.

of prolonged sacrifice beginning with the Great Depression and continuing throughout the war. Ironically, there had been far greater sacrifices made in Britain which had suffered the destruction that America had been spared, and Britain's economic recovery was far slower – rationing, for example, was still in effect for a number of years even after the armistice. Nevertheless, the image of British elegance prevailed, and this stylish pair of ships continued to monopolize the transatlantic trade for 20 years to come. For reasons of publicity rather than slowness, the *Queen Elizabeth* never captured the Blue Riband from her sister ship. The company preferred to refer to the *Queen Mary* as 'the fastest' and the *Queen Elizabeth* as 'the largest' ships ever to sail the Atlantic, rather than to encourage inter-company rivalry of the kind experienced by the German lines in the past.

By 1949, the 50 million dollars in revenue that the United States government estimated these two ships were earning for Great Britain became a source of great envy, since the majority of it came from American tourists headed east to see the European countries they had only read about during the war. The paradox of this

situation, in the heady years between the armistice and the end of this turbulent decade, was that such revenues were achieved in spite of growing competition from the airlines, whose capacity and range had increased dramatically in the empirical crucible of war. As Tom Hughes has said: 'Up to September 1939, air competition was non existent. After the war it was a dramatically different story. North Atlantic traffic statistics, published by the International Air Transport Association in June 1952, showed that member lines had carried 252,864 passengers in 1948, 272,637 in 1949, 317,164 in 1950 and 341,523 in 1951. In other words, over these four years, 1,184,188 passengers had preferred to save time by travelling by air rather than by sea. In ever increasing numbers they continued to do so.'

In the meantime, in the late forties and early fifties, an unmitigated preference for assured luxury, over the questionable safety and spartan conditions of early airliners, continued to hold sway; and the years from 1947 to 1957 were the most profitable decade in Cunard's history – traversing the Atlantic by ship remained 'the only way to cross'. The measure of that success may be gauged by the long list of distinguished and famous passengers carried during that time, including Queen Elizabeth, now the Queen Mother, who made several crossings on both the *Queen Mary* and *Queen Elizabeth*. She is remembered by both ships' crews for her particular interest in them, and in seeing life behind the scenes, beyond the metal doors that separated those serving and those served. The Duke of Windsor, formerly King Edward VIII, along with the Duchess, were also frequent passengers, as were many other heads of state, including Winston Churchill who continued to patronize the *Queen Mary* in peacetime. These passengers particularly valued the large outboard suites amidships on the main deck, for their security, spaciousness and privacy, as well as for their ability to accommodate a large entourage. The list of film stars that travelled on the *Queen Mary* both before and after the war is equally

Right Her Majesty Queen Elizabeth is introduced to the *Queen Mary*'s officers on one of the many post-war voyages on the ship.

Opposite page The Duke and Duchess of Windsor stroll on the sun deck as the *Queen Mary* prepares to sail.

caused was particularly harmful, in terms both of goodwill and future passengers lost to the airborne competition.

In an accident reminiscent of the brief grounding that had taken place as she left her fitting-out berth on the Clyde, the *Queen Mary* ran aground again near Cherbourg in October 1948, and was immediately returned to Southampton for temporary repair until her annual dry dock. The damage was extensive enough to require a patch and, as a precaution-ary measure, 100 tons of concrete was placed in the after end, just as it had been in the bow following the collision with the *Curacoa* six years before.

Labour issues caused difficulties again in February 1953. With tugboats and the docking pilot of New York harbour on strike, Cunard officials asked Captain Donald Sorrell if he could possibly manage without them, to which he replied: 'I will be delighted'. It was a Herculean task. Normally four or five tugboats were required to dock the *Queen Mary*.

long, and includes such names as Marlene Dietrich, Fred Astaire, Bob Hope, Clark Gable, Charlie Chaplin, David Niven, Gloria Swanson, Stan Laurel and Oliver Hardy. The noted American architect Frank Lloyd Wright also made the crossing to England in 1950, although his comments on the ship's decor sadly went un-recorded. Few of these celebrities lost the chance for a 'photo opportunity' while on board or arriving in port, posing in front of anything that might suitably convey an impression of first-class nautical panache.

These golden years were not, however, without incident. On 30 August 1947, barely one month after the first post-war run, a former German prisoner of war, Martin Georg Eppich, success-fully stowed away on the eastward journey to Southampton and, as one of the few to ever do so, served as a reminder that the liner had been used to transport his compatriots in the other direction only a short time before. In November of the same year, some of the crew struck in sympathy with a strike at the Merseyside docks. Considering that the ship was within 100 passengers of being at maximum capacity, the full day's delay that the strike

Opposite page The great American architect Frank Lloyd Wright strides purposefully on the *Queen Mary*'s sun deck.

Left Sir Winston Churchill in the *Queen Mary*'s drawing room.

Below Noël Coward poses in his stateroom.

Her four massive 35-ton propellers were intended to power the ship at high speeds on the open sea – they were not designed to manœuvre the giant liner in close quarters, where mere inches meant the difference between success and disaster. The docking process was further complicated by the slow-moving but powerful current of the Hudson River.' Using a home-made sighting device consisting of nails in a block of wood, Captain Sorrell was able to get the ship's bow past the pier, but a surge of current caught the stern, turning the bow towards the West Side Highway. As newspapers around the world were soon to proclaim, 'Spectators crowding the dock hurriedly moved back, expecting the worst. On the bridge,

Opposite page Clockwise from top left Marlene Dietrich clutches her hat as she poses for a mid-ocean photograph on the windy sports deck; Douglas Fairbanks Jnr and Norma Shearer dance in the verandah grill; Stan Laurel and Oliver Hardy; Bob Hope eyes Loretta Young upon arrival at Southampton in 1947 – fellow travellers are the actor Robert Montgomery, actress Alexis Smith and her husband Craig Stevens.

Left David Niven improvises a Highland Fling on the sports deck.

Below The actor Francis L Sullivan watches an impromptu boxing bout between two crew members staged for the benefit of cabin-class passengers.

Cunard

Captain Sorrell instantly recognized the danger and ordered the quartermaster, "All astern". Just in time, the ship moved back from the dock to mid channel. Sorrell decided to try again... Using the ship's lines and docking equipment, he brought the *Queen Mary* into dock on his second attempt, calmly telling the quartermaster, "All stop. Finished with engines".' It was a feat of immense skill.

Captain Sorrell was himself the cause of a strike when the Queen Mother chose to return to Britain on the *Queen Mary* in November 1954. Cunard seems to have misjudged his popularity with his crew, and was surprised by the strong reaction to its attempt to have a higher ranking Commodore preside over this voyage. Labour relations continued increasingly to plague the line throughout the mid-fifties, as indicated by an attempt by an assistant steward to sabotage the ship in 1956. He had managed to set the wood panelling in the observation lounge on fire before being caught and confined to quarters, narrowly escaping jail after a hearing in the Southampton Police Court, where he was fined twenty pounds.

Above A waiter flambés a dish as expectant diners look on.

Right Dinner in the main restaurant in the 1950s; the *Queen Mary*'s restaurant could accommodate all of the ship's 800 cabin-class passengers at a single sitting.

R.M.S. "QUEEN MARY"   Monday, January 12, 1959

BREAKFAST

Juices: Orange   Prune   Tomato
Oranges   Chilled Grape Fruit   Apples
Chilled Cavaillon Melon
Compote of Prunes   Baked Apples   Stewed Figs
Rolled Oats   Cream of Wheat   Oatmeal Porridge
Corn Flakes   Grape Nuts   All Bran   Rice Krispies
Sugar Pops   Bemax   Shredded Wheat   Sugar Smacks
Speciality: Onion Soup, Gratinée
Fried Fillets of Fresh Haddock, Rémoulade Sauce
Broiled Kippered Herrings
Eggs: Fried, Boiled, Poached and Scrambled
Omelettes (to order): Cheese, Mushroom, Jelly and Parmentier
Broiled American, Danish, Irish and Wiltshire Bacon
Minced Chicken on Waffle
Grilled Ham Slice, Chutney Sauce   Cambridge Sausages
Purée Potatoes
COLD: Rolled Ox Tongue   Boiled American Ham
Hearts of Lettuce   Radishes
Waffles, Buckwheat and Griddle Cakes
Maple and Golden Syrup
Breads: Sultana   Hovis   Carmalt   French   Corn   Brioche
Toast   Rye   Toasted English Muffins   Currant Scones
Croissants   White and Wholemeal Rolls   Danish Pastries
Hot Breakfast Biscuits
Preserves, Various   Honey   Marmalade
Teas: Ceylon   China
Instant Coffees: Postum   Nesrafé   Sanka   Chase and Sanborn
Ovaltine   Coffee   Chocolate   Cocoa   Yogurt
Horlick's Malted Milk   Fresh Milk
Passengers on Special Diet are especially invited to make known their
requirements to the Head Waiter
Speciality Foods for Infants are available on request

R.M.S. "QUEEN MARY"   Friday, August 9, 1957

DINNER

Pineapple Juice

Chilled Grape Fruit

Hors d'Œuvre:
Choux-fleurs, Portugaise   Herrings in Tomato   Anchovy Fillets
Œuf, Rémoulade   Primeurs à l'Huile   Pâte de Foie sur Croûte
Salade Parmentier

Consommé Sarah Bernhardt   Crème Montorgeuil

Grilled Fillets of Whitefish, Mirabeau
Suprême of Halibut, Vin Blanc

Spaghetti au Gratin

Braised Smoked Ox Tongue, Florentine

Roast Ribs and Sirloin of Beef, Horseradish Cream

GRILL: Calf's Liver, Fines-Herbes
French Beans   Squash Mornay
Boiled and Roast Potatoes

COLD: Roast Leg and Shoulder of Lamb, Mint Sauce
Spiced Ham

Salads: Chicory   Clover Club   Beetroot
Cream and Roquefort Dressings

Crème Suisse

Ice Cream: Vanilla   Pineapple
Apples   Pears   Oranges

Coffee

Red and White Bordeaux — per Bottle or en Carafe, 7/6; per glass, 1/3

Passengers on Special Diet are especially invited to make known their
requirements to the Chief Tourist Steward

Speciality Foods for Infants are available on request

Above left Dinner is served in the verandah grill in the late 1950s. Elements of this room's pre-war decor have survived, but its gold and silver colour scheme has been replaced with a uniform white.

Above Two luncheon menus from the mid-1960s; the leaning tower of Pisa was a favourite decorative theme.

Below left Breakfast and dinner menus from the late 1950s; passengers on a special diet were requested to make known their requirements to the head waiter, and a surcharge was made for wines and spirits.

Above Evening entertainment on the *Queen Elizabeth*.

Above right An invitational programme for a concert of songs and light music given by Robert Earl and the *Queen Mary* Concert Orchestra, dating from 1964.

Below right A Cunard brochure from the 1950s, encouraging American tourists to travel on the *Queen Mary* and *Queen Elizabeth* to Europe.

Opposite page After-dinner party games in the verandah grill.

David Marlowe, who had served on the *Queen Mary* in a similar capacity during the first few years of operation prior to the war, wrote a vivid account of the steward's lot in a newspaper article in 1937, and did not make it out to be a happy one. In it, he relates how quickly his pride at serving on 'the winner of the Blue Ribbon (sic) for England' and 'the finest liner that had ever been known', had changed to resentment at the work schedule he was expected to follow. Chief among his complaints were the bruises and exhaustion brought on by what seemed the incessant loading of the ship's stores, carried out during the 24-hour turnaround in New York and 48-hour stop-over in Southampton. His recollections bring home the reality of the tons of meat, fish, potatoes, vegetables, eggs, flour, sugar, milk, fruit, wine and spirits so cavalierly represented by the Cunard publicity department in graphic posters showing it all lined up along a dock to emphasize the ship's magnitude. While cranes performed the majority of the loading, the stewards were there when the sacks and crates descended and were expected to move them to the enormous cold storage rooms on the port side of D deck. Judging from David

Marlowe's description, cranes were a rare luxury, requiring stewards to pick the stores up from the dock, and carry them over a gang plank, in heavily laden human chains that moved back and forth from the ship all day. 'For hours,' he recalls, 'I had strained and panted my way up and down the sharply inclined gangway with heavy bags of linen, huge boxes of fish, sacks of potatoes. Sharp edges of boxes had cut hard into my shoulders, my hands were puffed and swollen. After that the milk arrived – some 300 huge urns ... we each grasped one handle of an urn and thus linked together proceeded slowly aboard. If the leader went too fast, your arms were extended at full length. Too slow, and the sharp edges of the urns cut into your ankles. After lunch we returned to find a railway van loaded with meat awaiting us. Under the crippling weight of a side of beef I staggered aboard ... and so it went on all day.'

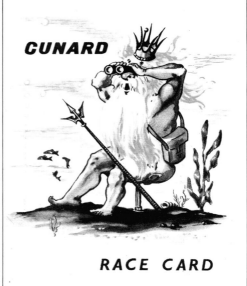

CUNARD

RACE CARD

HORSE RACING

First Race: "QUEEN MARY" MILE
Flat Race (5 dice)

1—ALWAYS IN ORDER	by Never out of Place
2—BROKEN WINDOW	by Eva Brick out of Space
3—NO HOPE	by Partner out of Trumps
4—WE KNOW	by Uno out of Player
5—GIMME	by Exchequer out of Profits
6—KEPT GOING	by Cheerfulness out of Hard Times

Second Race: ATLANTIC STEEPLECHASE
Hurdle Race (5 dice)

1—" HOW "	by Salutation out of Indian Chief
2—" WHO "	by Doctor out of B.B.C.
3—" NO "	by Doctor out of 007
4—RUINATION	by No Lead out of Trumps
5—DEPRESSION	by Packing out of Muddle
6—GLISTEN	by Toenail out of Sandal

Third Race: AMERICAN TWO MILE
Flat Race (2 dice)

1—DISTURBANCE	by Scientist out of Atom
2—STALEMATE	by Quack-Quack out of Conference
3—ANTICIPATION	by Traveller out of Coming Events
4—NEW CAR	by Few out of Patience
5—WOT!	by No Interest out of Stock
6—CASH	by May Be out of Finance Regulations

Fourth Race: OCEAN STAKES HANDICAP
Hurdle Race (5 dice)

1—BACHELOR	by Not Yet out of Nil Desperandum
2—MA-IN-LAW	by Welcome out of I Don't Think
3—SPINSTER	by Hope out of Leap Year
4—EAGLE	by Lair out of Rough
5—HAVE ANOTHER	by Good Fellow out of Bar
6—PREDICAMENT	by Good Fellow out of Cash

RULES

1—The Races will be run on the throw of Dice (weighted Dice not allowed).
2—A Horse will be disqualified and its Owner warned-off if it:—
    (a) Kicks or jostles another Horse during the Race;
    (b) Hangs on to the tail of the leading Horse;
    (c) Acts in any way unbecoming to its pedigree.
3—Ten per cent. of the Tote to Marine Charities.
4—Only authorised Bookies allowed on the Course.
5—The Judge must not disqualify any Horse in order to allow his own to win.

IF TIME PERMITS, A FIFTH RACE WILL BE RUN

PARI - MUTUEL BETTING

RC4—   R.M.S. "QUEEN MARY"

Opposite page above The bizarre spectacle of horse-racing at sea. This photograph was taken on board the *Queen Mary* just before the outbreak of war, but the practice resumed and was common throughout the 1950s and 1960s. Progress was dependent on the throw of dice and seamen or stewards would be on hand to move the wooden horses.

Opposite page below left and right A race card from the mid-1960s.

Left Recreational and sporting pursuits were an obvious way of passing the time at sea: passengers cavort in the *Queen Mary*'s cabin-class pool in the 1950s. The mosaic-lined balustrade seen here replaced the faience original which was removed during the war.

Below left Exercising in the *Queen Elizabeth*'s gymnasium.

Below right The *Queen Mary*'s first eleven for the 1952–53 soccer season.

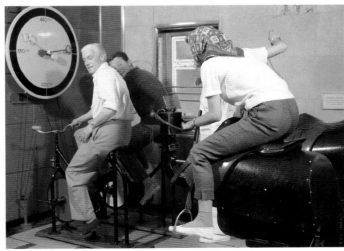

Above right Revellers watch at
the rail as the *Queen Mary* docks
in New York.

Below Events programmes
from the *Queen Mary*'s 1963–64
winter cruise season; perennial
favourites included fancy costume
balls, card parties, tea dances,
horse racing and bingo. Special
events were organized for
children.

Opposite page Father and son
look down on reclining passengers from their vantage point
on the raised promenade deck.

Once the stores were stowed away, the stewards'
more normal routine began, beginning at 6am
on the day of departure, scrubbing decks, floors
and staircases, and setting tables before the arrival
of the passengers, whose luggage would have to
be carried to their cabins. After serving lunch,
and washing dishes and cleaning the silver, there
was more baggage to be carried for those
departing at Cherbourg, on the outboard run,
followed by tea, which was served at 4pm, and
dinner beginning two hours later. Stewards ate
after the passengers had finished, typically

standing in the pantry, according to Marlowe,
since there was rarely enough time to go down
to the crew's galley on D deck to do so. After
eating, duties in the evening were split between
washing up in the kitchen or serving drinks in
one of the several lounges and smoking rooms,
before descent to the stewards' quarters which
was christened 'the Glory Hole', at the end of an
18-hour work day. 'It was,' Marlowe relates, 'the
hardest job of sheer non-stop labour that I have
ever known ... At times I did not know what day
it was, for each was so long and like another.
Weary and worn out, my feet swollen, tired to
my bones, I just carried on, cursing the vibration
that stole the few hours of sleep from me,
dreaming only of the time when I could get
off the ship.'

While the reminiscences of other crew members
include some more favourable memories, including expressions of regret that they ever had to
leave the ship at all, complaints about vibration in
the crew's quarters seem universal, and a 70 mph
gale in March 1956 brought the problem to the
passengers' attention as well. Over and above
the usual trembling, which travellers had come
to accept, this particular gale caused nearly 100
reported injuries split almost equally among passengers and crew alike, including many broken
bones. As a result, in 1958, Cunard finally
decided to take the *Queen Mary* temporarily out
of service in order to install Denny-Brown
stabilizers, a long and difficult process that took
nearly 18 months.

Marlowe's legitimate complaints about the steward's lot notwithstanding, the fact remains that
those who signed on were aware that it was not a
conventional job, and were usually well rewarded
for their efforts, at the end of each crossing.
While tips varied, according to where a steward
was assigned to work, it was possible for his
income to exceed the captain's, and it was not
uncommon, at the time of the *Queen Mary*'s
maiden voyage, for a good deck steward to make
£300 on each trip. Stewards' jobs were jealously
guarded, and passed on to relatives or friends,

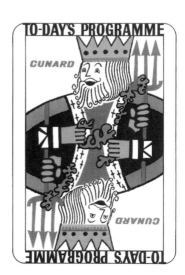

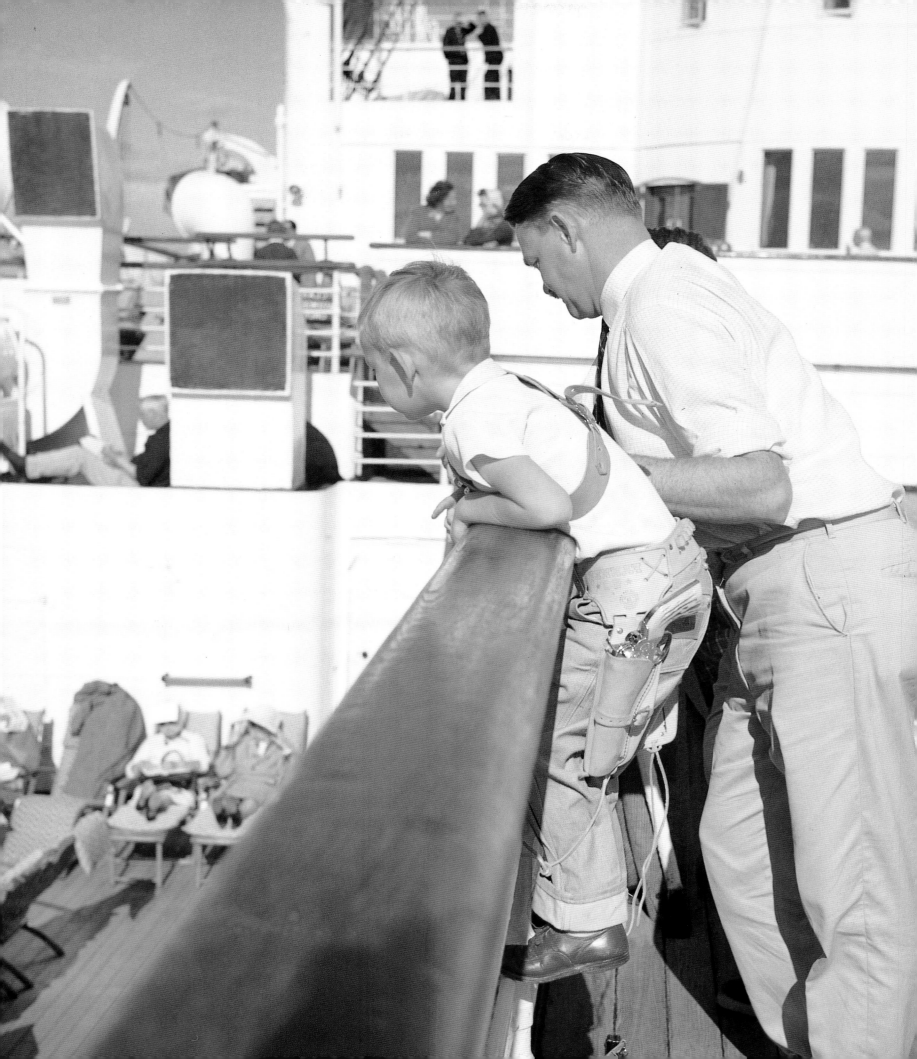

Above Passengers relax on the *Queen Mary*'s promenade deck in the 1950s.

as are those by waiters in first-class restaurants today, where income from tips is sizeable.

The trip from New York was typically the most lucrative, since American tourists, who have never been known to be stingy, were then most generous with cash, which was more scarce on their return from Europe. For every steward who found the social inequality all around him to be demeaning, there were many others who thrived on the routine and welcomed the economic benefit that it provided for the hard work demanded of them.

By 1958, post-war euphoria and the rush across the Atlantic that it had engendered had abated, and all North Atlantic passenger services, including Cunard's, began slowly to operate at a loss, due to the increasing competition from the airlines. Between the end of World War II and 1957, over one million passengers had crossed the North Atlantic by ship. Over the next eight years, only 650,000 would do so, while in the same period passenger traffic by air would increase from one million to four million per year. With

both Queens showing signs of wear, and creeping obsolescence, Cunard, in 1958, estimated that they would each have to be replaced by 1963. Estimating that a new ship, or pair of ships, would take three years to build, the company began agonizing over the decision involving the commissioning of one or two ships, which they calculated would cost upwards of £30 million each, and would probably continue to run at a loss. When questioned by the press on the matter in 1959, Colonel Fred Bates, a Cunard director, said he was 'content to let the jets take the new utility traffic' across the Atlantic, implying that the potential loss had been calculated in the new economic equation, and that the result, when weighed against the contribution the liners had made to British prestige, should be borne. Following the General Election in September of that year, the new Prime Minister Harold Macmillan said, 'we obviously must have the Queen liners', but confusion remained as to whether this meant keeping the *Queen Mary* and *Queen Elizabeth* in service indefinitely, or building two new liners to replace them.

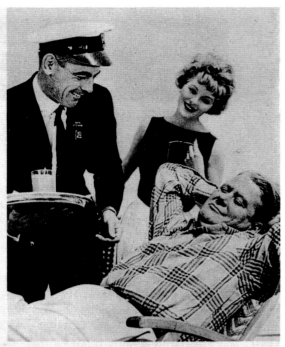

SAIL CUNARD TO ALL EUROPE

The largest passenger fleet on the Atlantic

FROM NEW YORK	FROM CANADA
QUEEN ELIZABETH	CARINTHIA
QUEEN MARY	CARMANIA
MAURETANIA	FRANCONIA
CARONIA	
SYLVANIA	

CRUISE CUNARD

Cunard has a year-round program of vacation cruises on 5 great cruise liners—

CARONIA
QUEEN ELIZABETH
CARMANIA
FRANCONIA
MAURETANIA

THE CUNARD STEAM-SHIP CO LTD

America further complicated the issue by fielding a liner of its own, the *United States*, which cost 79 million dollars and captured the Blue Riband on her maiden voyage in July 1952, making the crossing from New York to Southampton in three days ten hours and 40 minutes at an average speed of 35.59 knots, ten hours better than the *Queen Mary*'s fastest time. The glamour of the new liner drew passengers away from Cunard's tandem pair, not least of whom were the Duke and Duchess of Windsor who had become so closely identified with the *Queen Mary*. The speed of the *United States* raised the stakes and expectations surrounding any replacements that might be proposed by Cunard – even nuclear power was considered as a possibility. By 1960, a replacement for the *Queen Mary*, referred to as Q3 by Cunard officials, was openly discussed, with a cost estimated to be £30 million of which £18 million was expected as a subsidy; and governmental agreement was announced on 11 October. Opposition to the arrangement, however, primarily in the form of an effective letter-writing campaign directed at Cunard

shareholders, forced the postponement of a replacement for the *Queen Mary*. One month after the official agreement to subsidize a replacement had been announced to the press, the *Queen Mary* arrived from New York with only 437 passengers on board, or 20 per cent capacity.

By 1966, Cunard's woes, including a second attempt at arson by another disgruntled steward, were again compounded by a strike, of far greater severity than before. As Leslie Reade has described: 'The Prime Minister, Harold Wilson, begged the National Union of Seamen not to strike and the shipowners' Shipping Federation called the seamen "totally unreasonable" in their demand for a 17 per cent increase on top of 13 per cent in 1965. Captain Treasure Jones admitted the seamen had a case over the seven-day week, but he asserted the *Queen Mary* crew struck "with regret"... Her passage of 26 May was cancelled and her passengers were offered accommodation in foreign ships or by air. She and the *Queen Elizabeth* were strike-bound at Southampton and the Cunard

Above A 1964 advertisement for Cunard's transatlantic and cruising services.

Experts

to pamper you ..

Because truly fine service is a rarity in this modern age, you'll remember it as the crowning delight of your Cunard crossing. The personal warmth and sincerity of the smiling men and women...experts all...who serve you during the voyage are qualities born of pride in one's calling . . . a job well done. Service aboard a Cunarder is never given grudgingly...it springs from a century-old Cunard tradition . . . an honest, considerate desire to help make your voyage one of the most pleasurable experiences of your lifetime.

Service in a proud tradition

Opposite page Stewardesses and female staff line up for a group portrait on the *Queen Mary*'s promenade deck.

Left Service remained a Cunard byword, and gave the transatlantic ships their greatest advantage over the new breed of airliner.

two-ship weekly service, temporarily at least, had become no more than a public and international inconvenience.'

The company's annual report in 1966, revealed that the two ships were losing a total of £3 million annually and had been doing so for five years. The strike, it also noted, had cost the company £330,000 a week, or a total of nearly £2 million in the six weeks it had continued. A compromise, reached over the commissioning of a new ship, to be built by John Brown, already designated job number *736* – the future *Queen Elizabeth 2* – offered little solace to the company and its shareholders. A recurrence of vibration in the *Queen Mary*, due to a cracked propeller, and a costly refit of over one million pounds for the *Queen Elizabeth*, early in 1967, proved to be the final straw, in spite of valiant attempts over the previous two years to regain a portion of lost income by sending the Queens on winter-season

Above right Strikes dogged the *Queen Mary* and *Queen Elizabeth* throughout the 1950s and 1960s as this headline from the *Daily Sketch* of 2 April 1957 testifies.

Right The *Queen Mary* heading eastward beneath the Verrazano Narrows Bridge in the late 1960s as her career was drawing to a close.

cruises to the Bahamas to take advantage of the growing tourist market. The chairman of Cunard, Sir Basil Smallpeice, announced on 9 May 1967, that the *Queen Mary* would be permanently withdrawn from service in the autumn of that year, and the *Queen Elizabeth* would follow 12 months later. The captain of the *Queen Mary*, William Law, had been informed of the decision by confidential correspondence one day earlier. Speculation over the future of the two liners began almost immediately, with schemes for the *Queen Mary* ranging from the housing of London's homeless, to using her as the flagship of a service between Southampton and Sydney, before bids started coming in from New York, Philadelphia, and Long Beach, California. To everyone's surprise on 24 July 1967, tiny Long Beach was finally able to mount the successful offer.

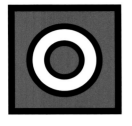n 16 September 1967 the *Queen Mary* set out from Southampton on her 1,000th Atlantic voyage and her last crossing to New York. As she slipped away from the Ocean Terminal, the decision was being made that would seal her fate. Many proposals had been

received by Cunard but rejected as either impractical or commercially competitive. Finally, a sealed-bid auction was won by oil-rich Long Beach, California with an offer of 3.45 million dollars. Her new owners proposed using her as a hotel, which was ironically appropriate considering her lineage as the product of a hotel designer's imagination.

Opposite The California sun blazes down on the *Queen Mary* throwing the details of her immense hull into sharp relief.

Right A ticket for the *Queen Mary* guided tour promising a 'behind the scenes look at the grandest ship ever built'.

An often-repeated axiom, frequently quoted whenever the *Queen Mary* was being compared to the *Normandie* in the halcyon days before the war, was that 'the French have built a beautiful hotel and put a ship around it, but the British have built a beautiful ship and put a hotel inside it'. This was to take on a new meaning in the *Queen Mary*'s final metamorphosis. But, before it could take place, officials from Long Beach, in meetings with Cunard, asked the company to organize one final cruise en route to their city, so that the ship, full of passengers as it had been at the height of its popularity, could be greeted with a gala reception when it arrived. They were so adamant on this point that they made it a condition of acceptance of their bid, with little appreciation of the difficulties that such a stipulation posed for Cunard.

The logistics of handling a full complement of passengers on the normal, North Atlantic route were difficult enough, in spite of administrative familiarity with the majority of problems that could occur, but the uncertainties of a 14,000-mile trip around Cape Horn, which was necessary because the *Queen Mary*'s size was too great to allow her to navigate the Panama Canal, would prove to be a nightmare and the Cunard officials knew it. Previous passages across the equator during the war, had resulted in extreme discomfort and many medical emergencies, due to the non-uniformity of the ship's air-conditioning system. But, regardless of Cunard's protests, the Long Beach delegation insisted on a final voyage, and so it was agreed to schedule it for 31 October 1967. The route that was finally determined included seven stop-overs before the final mooring at Long Beach: at Lisbon in Portugal, Las Palmas on the Canary Islands, Rio de Janeiro in Brazil, Valparaiso in Chile, Callas in Peru, Balboa in Panama and Acapulco in Mexico. In the event, despite extensive public relations efforts, only 1,200 passengers signed up for this 'farewell sailing'. Many had perhaps been dissuaded by Cunard's warnings that conditions aboard ship during the cruise would be warm, and rough, as the ship rounded the Horn. Those that did sail

included many regulars, who wanted to say a proper 'goodbye'. Others simply saw this as an opportunity to participate in history in the making, or were attracted by the possibility of a non-stop party that promised to last longer than a month. The minimum price for two was £395.

The *Queen Mary* returned from her last eastward passage from New York on Wednesday, 27 September having covered 3,044 miles in four days, 13 hours and 15 minutes, through gale-force winds. In the midst of squalls and heavy swells, the two sister ships passed each other for the last time in mid-Atlantic just after midnight on 25 September, Commodore Geoffrey Marr at the helm of the *Queen Elizabeth*, and Captain Treasure Jones guiding the *Queen Mary*. Many passengers stayed up to witness this passing, mindful that in the few minutes it took to transpire, an era had ended. One participant, who regularly travelled on the *Queen Mary* recalled that, in marked contrast to other meetings there were no whistles, shouts or salutes that night, and that people tended to stand alone or in small groups, protected from the wind by the shelter of the promenade deck, looking on in silence as the two ships passed. Southampton greeted the *Queen Mary* with a huge public turnout including a military band and, ironically, a dockworkers' strike, which seems an appropriate coda to this troubled period of the ship's history; earlier strikes which had plagued her final years contributed significantly to the *Queen Mary*'s demise. This was the last official voyage, the 1,001st that the *Queen Mary* made, completing 31 years of service, during which she had sailed more than 3,795,000 miles and carried more than 2,115,000 fare-paying passengers.

A little over one month later, with 1,040 American passengers on board, the *Queen Mary* left Southampton for the last time, from berth 107 in the Western Docks rather than her customary pier in the Ocean Terminal, to the accompaniment of 'Auld Lang Syne' played by the Royal Marine Band; 14 navy helicopters flew above in an anchor-formation salute.

Opposite Shortly after midnight on 25 September 1967, the *Queen Elizabeth* passed the *Queen Mary* at sea for the last time. Commodore Geoffrey Marr of the *Queen Elizabeth* sent this radiogram to Captain Treasure Jones.

Overleaf The *Queen Mary* leaves New York on 22 September 1967 never to return. A 310-foot paying-off pennant (ten feet for every 31 years of service) billows from her mast.

Pages 230–231 The *Queen Mary* enters Long Beach Harbour on 9 December 1967.

226

RADIOGRAM

CUNARD STEAM-SHIP CO. LTD.

RADIO SERVICES OPERATED BY

INTERNATIONAL MARINE RADIO CO., LTD.

Received by R.M.S. "QUEEN MARY"   Date....24/9/67........   Form B.52M
Printed in England

PREAMBLE:	PREFIX	OFFICE OF ORIGIN NUMBER	NO. OF WORDS	DATE	TIME	SERVICE INSTRUCTIONS		
RADIO:	MSG	QUEEN ELIZABETH	N/C	24				

TO	CAPTAIN TREASURE JONES		RECEIVED		
	QUEEN MARY		FROM	TIME	BY
			GBSS	1452Z	JW

YOU can telephone or telegraph to any part of the world from this ship. You can thus use the radio service to reply to this message, to reserve accommodation on shore, and make railway and aeroplane reservations from mid-ocean in advance of your arrival.

You can also communicate with your home or business at any time during the voyage.

Enquiries respecting this message should be made at the International Marine Radio Co. Ltd's Radio Office on board, or addressed to the International Marine Radio Co. Ltd., Peall Road, Croydon, Surrey, and must be accompanied by this form.

Please read on the back of this form the conditions under which this message has been transmitted.

COMMEMORATING VESSEL'S LAST VOYAGE

CHIEF RADIO OFFICER

1400Z POS 4938N 3005W CO 259 SPEED 27.5 KTS WIND NW 6 BARO 996
CLOUDY AND CLEAR WE HAD A BIT OF A BLOW YESTERDAY JUST OFF IRELAND
BUT IT LOOKS AS IF THOUGH YOU SHOULD HAVE FOLLOWING WINDS .
IT IS A SAD MOMENT AS THESE TWO GREAT SHIPS PASS FOR THE LAST TIME
BUT WE HOPE TO SEE YOU SHORTLY AFTER MIDNIGHT NEW TIME AND MOST OF
MY PASSENGERS ARE WAITING UP FOR THIS HISTORIC EVENT HOPE THAT
YOU AND YOUR WIFE ENJOY THE TRIP ROUND CAPE HORN REGARDS AND BEST
WISHES

GEOFFREY

Above The route of the *Queen Mary's* last and possibly longest voyage, 14,559 miles from Southampton to Long Beach via Cape Horn.

Recollections of the trip that was to follow vary, but there is general agreement that the initial reservations expressed by Cunard officials were borne out. As Leslie Reade has described: 'The tropical heat over long glaring days and sweating nights made life unpleasant for the passengers, and worse than that for the crew in their maritime equivalent of Edwardian servants' quarters. An assistant chef collapsed from the heat in his cabin, died and was buried at sea. There were complaints about the service. Only 860 instead of the usual 1,100 had signed on and so she was understaffed. Unknown to the passengers, a stiff argument between crew and management had taken the whole day previous to her sailing. A bonus of £25 had been offered for the voyage; the crew had asked for £75 and in the end had accepted £40, but there was considerable lack of enthusiasm in the service.'

In an attempt to economize further, Cunard decided that the ship would run on two rather than four propellers, in order to save fuel; restricting speed to a maximum of 20 knots. This decision eventually led to a shortening of the advertised length of stay in each of the seven ports en route, in order to arrive at Long Beach on schedule, causing further discontent among the passengers who began to leave early in protest. One couple, who left the ship at Rio de Janeiro and flew home to Long Beach, told the press that the *Queen Mary* was 'a nightmare of rats and cockroaches', a claim that was subsequently proved to be untrue. They were accompanied, at the same stop-over, by a woman who was forcibly evicted from the ship for soliciting for prostitution, which justifiably led one commentator to categorize the entire voyage as a 'pathetic travesty' of the *Queen Mary's* distinguished former career. This travesty was also perpetuated in other ways, such as the struggle for seats on the two double-decker London buses on the after end of main deck, which were destined for use in the theme park to be built around the ship's mooring at Long Beach, by those who wanted to claim that they had gone around Cape Horn on a bus. In the end, however, all of the

passengers who remained on board shared in superlatives of the kind that Cunard once loved to publicize: being on the largest ship, with the greatest number of passengers ever to round Cape Horn, and participating in the most demonstrative welcome the ship had ever received, once it reached Long Beach.

The *Queen Mary* finally arrived in Long Beach on 9 December 1967, after a 14,559-mile journey, 40 days after leaving Southampton. Five hundred miles off the California coast, a Douglas Aircraft DC-9 attempted a re-enactment of her maiden entry into New York harbour, when World War I ace Eddie Rickenbacker had scattered flowers over her from his DC-2; but this time the hundreds of carnations missed, landing in the water nearby. Photographs of the well-intentioned tribute, taken from another DC-9 nearby, graphically convey the insensitivity of this second gesture, not only in the miscalculated trajectory of the flowers, but also in dropping them from a jet at all, since it represented the competition that the *Queen Mary* had been pitted against since the end of World War II. Such symbolism was undoubtedly lost on the relieved passengers and crew as they approached their final destination, as well as on the 6,000 well-wishers who came out to greet the ship in a small armada of craft, from cabin cruisers to Coast Guard cutters, as tugs guided the vessel to Pier E in Long Beach Harbour. At 12.07pm, Captain Treasure Jones signalled, 'Finished with engines', for the last time from the bridge telegraph; and, two days later, formally handed the *Queen Mary* over to her new owners. The ship's register was officially transferred to the British Consul General, and from that date the *Queen Mary* was removed from the Register of Ships. Her propellers were disconnected from the engines and henceforward the *Queen Mary* was classified as a building.

For some strange reason, the most disturbing change of all those that have since taken place on the *Queen Mary*, regardless of the inestimable losses that she has suffered, in rooms such as the verandah grill, has been the alteration of her machinery, the source of her power. The single slowly-rotating propeller, seen through the hole in the hull, is a more moving reminder of what the ship once was than all of the empty public rooms, photographs and artefacts in its maritime museum, or hermetically-sealed vignettes of wartime crowding – precisely because it is so massive and so useless. Even though countless publicity shots issued by John Brown at the time of construction should theoretically alleviate the shock of its size, they in fact do not. There is something about the way the propeller has been presented, as if it were some rare type of enormous, endangered mammal trapped in a cage, that is unforgettable, a pointed reminder once again of the all-consuming importance of speed – the invisible barrier which the *Queen Mary* once conquered, and which ultimately conquered her. It requires no profound leap of imagination to quantify mentally the combined effect of four gigantic propellers rotating at full speed, and all of the proto-Homeric descriptions of them 'whipping the sea into a froth' and turning 'the brine into foam' suddenly seem quite plausible. Other associations also spring to mind: 1961, the year that the 'Q3' replacement for the *Queen Mary* was discarded by Cunard was the same year that another venerable British institution, Jaguar motor cars, introduced their 150 mph E-type sports car, which rapidly captured the public's imagination. Speed again, inextricably tied as it is to economics, remains as important as the idea of progress which has been transposed but not displaced as an equally important leveller; significantly, 1967, the *Queen Mary*'s last year of service, also saw the first test flight of the Anglo-French supersonic airliner *Concorde* which was to take transatlantic travel into a yet faster age.

In that sense, the useless, single propeller may provide the best clue yet to the relevance of the *Queen Mary* for us today, beyond the nostalgia for deck chairs and steamer blankets, moonlight on the water, brass and onyx, salt-water baths, boat trains and telegrams, stewards and bell boys, tea at four, silver trolleys holding large roasts of

beef and Yorkshire pudding, incandescent light shining on wood-veneer walls, and formal dress for dinner served at real tables, set with real linen, and real flowers, among the hundreds of other small details which have now passed into history. The lesson of the *Queen Mary* lies in the way that steel was shaped to create all of the parts which, when added up and riveted together make a ship, in a way robotics today could never match. The *real* artisans involved in this project were not listed in a publicity brochure for public consumption, but were the engineers and craftsmen at Clydebank who laid the keel, framed the hull, double-plated the bottom, cast the stem, riveted the shellplating, erected the superstructure, laid the decks, built and installed the rudder, honed the propellers, assembled the turbines blade-by-blade, prepared the wooden launching ways, and finally fitted her out. There is, amongst even the most cynical critics of the destruction wrought by the industrial revolution, a secret admiration for the hand-crafted precision of early machinery, for steam engines, and engineering masterpieces. The *Queen Mary* is the last tangible repository of the sum of all of that instinctive, visceral knowledge, as applied to the building of ships, stretching back to the *Britannia* built for Samuel Cunard, and to the *Great Britain*, designed by the pioneering engineer Isambard Kingdom Brunel, and famous as the first iron-hulled steamship to cross the North Atlantic.

Having escaped cancellation during the Depression, the threat of German submarines and bombing during World War II, collision with the *Curacoa*, a crushed stern from running aground, and several attempts at sabotage, the *Queen Mary* has miraculously eluded the destruction that befell her contemporaries and remains a testimony to the highest aspirations and talents of the age.

Below A special medal was struck to celebrate the *Queen Mary*'s arrival at Long Beach and to commemorate this final phase of her long career.

Thirty-three captains served on the *Queen Mary* during her 31 years of service. The names of the captains, with the date on which they first assumed command, are:

1 December 1935	Commodore Sir Edgar T Britten
29 January 1936	Captain George Gibbons
4 August 1936	Commodore Reginald V Peel
11 November 1936	Commodore Robert B Irving
30 March 1937	Captain John C Townley
19 April 1938	Captain Peter A Murchie
9 April 1941	Captain Ernest M Fall
23 February 1942	Commodore Sir James Bisset
10 August 1942	Commodore Cyril G Illingworth
29 July 1944	Captain Roland Spencer
11 March 1946	Commodore Chas M Ford
6 December 1946	Commodore George E Cove
15 February 1947	Commodore Sir C Ivan Thompson
6 March 1947	Captain John A MacDonald
4 July 1947	Captain John D Snow
31 December 1948	Commodore Harry Grattidge
20 July 1950	Captain Harry Dixon
13 August 1951	Captain Robert G Thelwell
19 August 1952	Captain Donald W Sorrell
27 June 1956	Commodore George G Morris
25 June 1957	Commodore Chas S Williams
11 September 1957	Captain Alexander B Fasting
26 August 1958	Captain Andrew MacKellar
22 October 1958	Commodore John W Caunce
24 June 1959	Commodore Donald M MacLean
30 March 1960	Captain James Crosbie Dawson
25 May 1960	Captain Sidney A Jones
9 August 1960	Commodore Frederick G Watts
19 June 1962	Captain Eric A Divers
7 May 1964	Commodore Geoffrey T Marr
8 September 1965	Captain John Treasure Jones
15 September 1965	Captain William E Warwick
3 May 1967	Captain William J Law

27 December 1930	Keel laid
12 December 1931	Work suspended due to economic emergency
December 1933	Government subsidy announced
3 April 1934	Work resumed
26 September 1934	Date launched
24 March 1936	Departure from Clydebank
26 March 1936	Arrival at Southampton
April 1936	Speed trials
27 May 1936	Maiden voyage from Southampton to New York
5 June 1936	Return voyage from New York
17 June 1936	Second sailing from Southampton
30 August 1939	Last pre-war sailing to New York
March 1940 – September 1946	War service
	War history: Carried a total of 765,429 military personnel. Sailed a total of 569,429 miles (916,407km). Carried wounded returning to the United States. Transported Winston Churchill three times to conferences. Carried 12,886 GI brides and children
31 July 1947	Resumed peacetime passenger service
19 September 1967	Retired from regular passenger service (after completing 1,001 crossings of the Atlantic)
Tuesday, 31 October 1967	Departed on 'Last Great Cruise'
Saturday, 9 December 1967	Arrived at Long Beach, California
10 am Monday, 11 December 1967	Change of ownership: Removed from British registry and officially turned over to ownership of City of Long Beach

Constructed by	John Brown and Company Limited, Clydebank, Scotland
Gross tonnage	81,237 gross tons
Overall length	1,019.5 feet
Moulded breadth	118 feet
Height	92.5 feet (from keel to promenade deck)
Draft	39 feet 4$^{9}/_{16}$ inches
Number of decks	12
Length of promenade deck	724 feet
Rudder	140 tons
Hull plates	8 to 30 feet in length; up to 1$^{1}/_{4}$ inches thick
Bow anchors	2 of 16 tons; 18 feet in height
Anchor chain	900 feet in length; weighing 45 tons. Anchor chain link: 2 feet long, weighing 224 lb
Whistles	3 – steam type; two on forward funnel, one on middle funnel, each over 6 feet long, weighing 2,205 lb
Lifeboats	24, powered by 18 hp diesel engines. Capacity: 145 persons
Smokestacks	3 – elliptical in shape; 36 feet fore and aft, 23.3 feet wide. Height: forward; 70.5 feet, middle: 67.5 feet, aft: 62.25 feet
Cruising speed	28.5 knots
Fuel consumption	13 feet per gallon
Passenger capacity	1,957
Officers and crew	1,174

S Nicholson Babb and Allan Howes

bronze statuettes in the main lounge

Charles Cameron Baillie

decorative glass in the tourist-class swimming bath; murals
and decorative glass in the third-class public rooms

Gilbert Bayes and Alfred J Oakley

panel in bas-relief at the fore end of the main lounge

A Duncan Carse

two decorative paintings in the restaurant

Philip Connard

large decorative painting in tapestry technique, depicting
English country life and scenes, at the after end of the
cabin-class restaurant (C deck)

Bainbridge Copnall

applied carvings on wood in the cabin-class restaurant (C deck)

Norman J Forrest

four statuettes in the vestibules to the tourist-class main
staircase

Margot Gilbert

decorative motifs painted on hide in the tourist-class lounge

Walter Gilbert and Donald Gilbert

cast bronze doors and illuminated medallions in the
cabin-class restaurant

MacDonald Gill

decorative map of the North Atlantic, with moving model
of the *Queen Mary*, in the cabin-class restaurant.

Jan Juta

two large panels in decorative glass on gold backgrounds in
the ballroom

**Dame Laura Knight, Agnes Pinder-Davis,
Vanessa Bell and H Davis Richter**

paintings in the private dining rooms

Maurice Lambert

modelled plaque in burnished phosphor-bronze over the
proscenium in the main lounge, also four metal motifs over
the forward and after entrance doors; plaster frieze in ivory
tone, 50 feet long, in front of the main outfitters' shop in
the main hall; two motifs in aluminium, symbolizing speed
and progress, on either side of the travel bureau

Cedric Morris

two flower-study paintings at each end of the starboard gallery

Algernon Newton

painting at the after end of the long gallery

Bertram Nicholls

painting of pastoral scenes at the forward end of the long gallery

Charles Pears

decorative painting in the tourist-class smoking room

Herry Perry

decorative map over the fireplace in the tourist-class
smoking room; wall decorations throughout the tourist-class
children's playroom

George Ramon

incised and painted designs on the walls of the cabin-class
children's playroom

Kenneth Shoesmith

decorative panel over the mantelpiece, paintings on panels
over the doors enclosing the altar and oil painting forming
reredos of altar in the cabin-class drawing room; two further
paintings in the tourist-class library

John Skeaping

three large mural carvings on the inboard wall of the
starboard gallery

Rebel Stanton

bas-reliefs in metal in the tourist-class lounge

Alfred R Thomson

mural painting over the cocktail bar in the observation lounge

Edward Wadsworth

two paintings at the forward and after ends of the cabin-class
smoking room

Tom Webster

frieze of sporting subjects in the gymnasium

James Woodford

three pierced and carved screens flanking the fireplace in
the port-side recess of the cabin-class smoking room, also
modelled symbolical figures in the dome of this room

Lady Hilton Young (Lady Kennett)

marble plaque of HM Queen Mary, set in a panel of
special walnut burr, at the head of the main staircase facing
the main hall

Anna Zinkeisen

murals on canvas in the ballroom

Doris Zinkeisen

canvas paintings in the verandah grill, also decorations to
the piers and mast in this room

REFERENCES

Full details of works cited will be found in the Bibliography

THE STATELIEST SHIP
Hughes, 1973.
Leigh-Bennett, 1934.
The Shipbuilder and Marine Engine Builder, special *Queen Mary* souvenir number, June 1936.
The Times, London, 27 September 1934.
Weekly Illustrated, special *Queen Mary* number, May 1936.

THE GLORY YEARS
Daily Mail, London, August 15 1938.
Daily Telegraph, special *Queen Mary* supplement, London, 25 May 1936.
Maguglin, 1991.
Maxtone-Graham, 1972
Reade, 1979.
The Shipbuilder and Marine Engine Builder, special *Queen Mary* souvenir number, June 1936.
The Times, London, 23 May 1936.
Waugh, Evelyn, *Brideshead Revisited*, London, 1945.

THE 'GREY GHOST'
Bisset, 1961.
Bryant, 1957.
Maxtone-Graham, 1972.
Reade, 1979.

FROM STRIPES TO STARS
Hughes, 1973.

CODA: VOYAGE 1002
Reade, 1979.

SELECT BIBLIOGRAPHY

Amory, Cleveland, *Who Killed Society?*, New York, 1960

Angas, W Mac, *Rivalry on the Atlantic, 1833–1939*, New York, 1939

Archibald, E H H, *Travellers by Sea*, London, 1962

Bailey, Chris Howard, *Down the Burma Road*, Southampton Maritime Museum, 1990

Beaver, Patrick, *The Big Ship*, London, 1969

Bisset, Commodore Sir James, *Commodore*, New York, 1961

Blake, George, *British Ships and Shipbuilders*, London, 1946

Bonsor, N R P, *North Atlantic Seaway; An Illustrated History of the Passenger Services Linking the Old World with the New*, London, 1955

Brinnin, John Malcolm, *The Sway of the Grand Saloon; A Social History of the North Atlantic*, Delacorte Press, New York, 1971

Brinnin, John Malcolm and Gaulin, Kenneth, *Grand Luxe: The Transatlantic Style*, Holt, New York, 1988

Bryant, Arthur, *The Turn of the Tide 1939–1943. A Study Based on the Diaries and Autobiographical Notes of Field Marshal The Viscount Alanbrooke*, London, 1957.

Cairis, Nicholas T, *North Atlantic Passenger Liners Since 1900*, London, 1972

Church, Robert F, *The Cunard Steamship Company Ltd*, Evanston III, Transportation Center at Northwestern University, 1968

Coleman, Terry, *The Liners: A History of the North Atlantic Crossing*, Putnam, New York, 1977

Cronican, Frank and Mueller, Edward A, *The Stateliest Ship*, New York, 1968

Cutler, Carl C, *Queens of the Western Ocean*, Annapolis, 1961

Dugan, James, *The Great Iron Ship*, London, 1953

Dunn, Laurence, *Passenger Liners*, Adlard Coles, London, 1965

Emmons, Frederick, *The Atlantic Liners, 1925–70*, Drake Publishers, New York, 1972

Emmons, Frederick, *American Passenger Ships: The Ocean Lines and Liners, 1873–1983*, University of Delaware Press; London; Cranbury, NJ, Associated University Presses, 1985

Ford, Hugh D, *Nancy Cunard: Brave Poet, Indomitable Rebel, 1896–1965*, Philadelphia, 1968

Frost, Jack, *The Queen Mary*, London, 1971

Gibbs, Commander C R Vernon, *RN Passenger Liners of the Western Ocean: A Record of the North Atlantic Steam and Motor Passenger Vessels from 1838 to the Present Day*, London, 1952

Gibbs, Commander C R Vernon, *RN Western Ocean Passenger Line and Liners 1934–1969*, Glasgow, 1970

Grant, Hilda, K, *Samuel Cunard, Pioneer of the Atlantic Steamship*, London, 1967

Grattidge, Captain Harry, *Captain of the Queens*, London, 1956

Hyde, Francis Edwin, *Cunard and the North Atlantic, 1840–1973: A History of Shipping and Financial Management*, Humanities Press, Atlantic Highlands, NJ, 1975

Hughes, Tom, *The Blue Riband of the Atlantic*, Cambridge, 1973

Kludas, Arnold, *Great Passenger Ships of the World, Volumes 1–5*, Cambridge, 1972–1974

Leigh-Bennett, E P, *Masterpiece in the Making: A Pen Picture of the Activity in the Yard Shortly Before the Launch*, published privately by Cunard White Star and John Brown Ltd in a booklet to commemorate the launch of the *Queen Mary*, September 1934.

Maguglin, Robert & Winberg, William, *Queen Mary: The Official Pictorial History*, California 1991

Marr, Commodore Geoffrey, *The Queens and I*, London, 1973

Maxtone-Graham, John, *The North Atlantic Run: The Only Way to Cross*, Cassell, London, 1972

Miller, Byron S, *Sail, Steam and Splendour: A Picture History of Life Aboard the Transatlantic Liners*, New York, 1977

Miller, William H, *The Great Luxury Liners, 1927–1954: A Photographic Record*, New York, 1981

Mitchell, Alan, *Splendid Sisters*, London, 1966

Newell, Gordon, *Ocean Liners of the 20th Century*, Seattle, 1963

Potter, Neil and Frost, Jack, *The Mary*, London, 1961 Randsome-Wallis, Patrick, *North Atlantic Panorama, 1900–1976*, Wesleyan University Press, Middletown, Conn, 1977

Reade, Leslie, Introduction and Epilogue to *Ocean Liners of the Past, Queen Mary, The Cunard White Star Quadruple-Screw North Atlantic Liner*, London and New York, 1979. Largely reprinted from special souvenir number of *The Shipbuilder and Marine Engine Builder*, June 1936

Smith, Eugene W, *Passenger Ships of the World Past and Present*, Boston, 1963

Wall, Robert, *Ocean Liners*, New York, 1977

Watton, Ross, *The Cunard Liner, Queen Mary; Anatomy of the Ship*, London, 1989

Winter, Ron, *Queen Mary: Her Early Years Recalled*, London and New York, 1986

Illustrations:
(key: t: top; c: centre; b: bottom;
l: left; r: right)
Peter Aprahamian: 4, 46bl, 93b,
99b, 118, 130, 138, 142, 224,
225t; Bridgeman Art Library:
163, fold-out; Cunard: 3tcl, 3tcr,
3tr, 5, 11t, 12t, 13, 15b, 18tl,
18tr, 19, 23, 24, 25, 32, 33tl, 34b,
36, 38t, 47, 54, 57, 70, 71, 77br,
89, 93t, 95, 99tr, 147, 152–3,
155, 161, 165, 210tl, 210bl,
211tr, 211cr, 211bl, 212, 215bl,
216bl, 216br, 217, 218l, 218r,
219, 221r, 227; ET Archives: 17tl,
17tr, 17bl; Philippe Garner: 16,
160, 162b; Hippodrome Gallery
(First reproduced in the *Art of
the RMS Queen Mary* by Douglas
M Hinkey): 2, 69c, 84, 87, 92t,
98, 100, 102b, 103, 105t, 106,
107, 108, 109, 110, 114, 115,
117, 119, 120, 121t, 122, 123br,
124br, 127r, 129t, 129r, 132tl,
133, 143, 144t, 145, 146, 157t,
162t; Angelo Hornak: 73t, 74t,
74br, 75; Imperial War Museum:
167t, 167c, 169, 172, 173r, 175,
178r, 179, 180b, 182tl, 182tr,
183bl, 183br; Kobal: 77bl;
Maxtone-Graham Collection: 6t,
11b, 69t, 77t, 80, 94b, 164, 166,
170, 186–7, 187tr, 192, 193t,
194–5, 198, 199t, 214t, 222–3,
228–9, 233; National Maritime
Museum: 171l; The Board of
Trustees of the National
Museum and Galleries on
Merseyside: 3bl, 3br, 221, 156–7,
196, 197, 208tl, 211br; 221;
Ocean Liner Museum, New
York: 204, 205b, 207t, 215t;
Range: 14t, 15t; RMS Foundation
Inc: 6–7b, 9, 10, 11c, 12b, 18b,
20, 21, 26–7, 28, 29b, 30, 31, 35,
37, 38b, 40–41, 42, 43, 44–5,
48–9, 50, 53, 56tl, 56br, 58, 59b,
60, 61, 62, 63, 64, 65, 66–7, 68,
74bl, 76, 78, 79, 81, 82–3, 85,
88, 90, 91, 92b, 94t, 101, 102tr,
104, 105b, 111, 116, 121b, 123t,
123bl, 124t, 124bl, 125, 126–7,
128, 129l, 131, 132tr, 132b, 134,
135, 136t, 137t, 137bl, 140, 141,
148tl, 148cl, 148bl, 148br, 149,
150, 151, 158–9, 167b, 168b,
173l, 174, 176, 177, 180t, 181,
182b, 183t, 184, 185, 188, 189,
190–91, 193c, 193b, 194l, 200,
201, 202, 203, 205t, 206, 207,
208–9, 210r, 211tl, 215br,
220–21, 222l, 225c, 225b,
230–31; Stapleton Collection:
17br, 99tl; Susan Tunick: 14b;
Archives Unit, University of
Liverpool: 3tl, 69b, 73b, 154,
168t, 199b, 213; Madame
Yevonde Archives: 59t, 86.
Jacket illustration by
Andrew Davidson.

Acknowledgements: The author
and publisher would like to
thank John Maxtone-Graham for
writing the foreword and for his
careful reading of the text.
Thanks also to Ronald L Smith,
Exhibits Coordinator of the RMS
Queen Mary; Cynthia B
MacMullin, Director of the
Hippodrome Gallery in Long
Beach; Julian Hill of the Queen
Mary Foundation in England;
William Winberg and Kay
Romer in Long Beach; the
University Archives in Liverpool;
Gordon Read at the Maritime
Museum in Liverpool and the
Head Archivist at the Mitchell
Library in Glasgow for their
assistance in research.

The author also acknowledges
the contribution of Jo Newson,
who assisted with the chapter
The 'Grey Ghost', and would like
to thank Sarah Castle, Kelly
Mullins and Sue Strakosch for
their help in the preparation of
the manuscript, and David
Pocknell, Leah Klein, Erica
Rosen, Polly Clayden,
Vivian Constantinopoulos and
David Jenkins at Phaidon for
making this book possible.

Phaidon Press Limited
Regent's Wharf
All Saints Street
London N1 9PA

First published 1995
Reprinted 1995, 1996

© 1995 Phaidon Press Limited

page 8: 'Number 534'
© 1934 John Masefield:
reprinted by permission of
The Society of Authors as the
literary representatives of
the Estate of John Masefield

pages 31–47: Extracts from
'Masterpiece in the Making'
© 1934 E P Leigh-Bennett

pages 144, 161: Extracts
from *Brideshead Revisited*
© 1945 Evelyn Waugh: reprinted
by permission of the Peters
Fraser and Dunlop Group Ltd

ISBN 0 7148 2891 2

A CIP catalogue record for
this book is available from the
British Library

Printed in Hong Kong